中国的故事 · 历史篇
STORIES FROM CHINA
History

中国文化阅读丛书
A Series on Chinese Culture

刘美如（Meiru LIU）吕丽娜（Lina LU）　编著
Ian Wollman　翻译

PHOENIX TREE PUBLISHING INC.

Published by Phoenix Tree Publishing Inc.

Stories from China: History
by Meiru LIU & Lina LU
ISBN: 978-1-62575-000-6
Library of Congress Control Number: 2013930375
First Edition
Second Printing: September 2016
Printed in China

Chinese Editors: Zhou Li & Wang Xuefei
English Editor: Hou Xiaojuan
Graphic Designer: Li Jia
Photo Credits: Microfotos（微图网）, frontfoto（前图网）
and CNSfoto（中国新闻图片网）

Phoenix Tree Publishing Inc.
5660 N. Jersey Ave · Chicago, IL 60659
Phone: 773.250.0707 · Fax: 773.250.0808
Email: marketing@phoenixtree.com

For information about special discounts for bulk purchases,
please contact the publisher at the address above.
Find out more about Phoenix Tree Publishing Inc. at
www.phoenixtree.com

编写说明

编写理念

◉ 语言教学和文化教学相结合

通过阅读本系列读物，使学习者在培养阅读技能的同时，对中国文化有更深入的认识和了解，培养、发展学生的国际视野和跨文化交际能力。

◉ 遵循海外本土汉语阅读教材的编写特点、发展趋势

我们的编写理念是建立在给学生"看什么"（阅读的内容）、"为什么看"（阅读原因）、"如何看"（阅读方法）的基础上的，注重教材的知识性、故事性、趣味性、实用性、适用性、可读性、易读性。每个故事均以启发学习者阅读兴趣的导读问题开始，增强互动性，更多地调动学生阅读前的思考，激发学生的阅读兴趣。

◉ 以国家标准和大纲为依据

本书在编写中参考了美国国家外语协会制定的《21世纪外语学习标准》，在文中贯穿五大原则目标，即沟通（Communication）、文化（Cultures）、贯连（Connections）、比较（Comparisons）和社区（Communities），使学习者通过使用本套教材，提高运用中文进行沟通的能力，充分认识、理解和掌握中国文化，并能将其贯连到其他专科领域，培养学习者比较不同语言文化之间特点的能力，并将其运用到日常生活和学习中。

在词汇控制方面，以中国国家汉办颁布的《新汉语水平考试大纲》和《汉语国际教育用音节汉字词汇等级划分》为依据，对语料进行加工，控制词汇难度。

◎ **以"通过阅读学会阅读"为目的**

在本系列读物的练习设计中，语言理解和课文理解两种形式的练习轻重并举、比重适量，避免过多的语法语义方面的练习，以保证阅读的趣味性，力求达到让学习者"通过阅读学会阅读"的根本目的。

适用对象

本套读物适合具有中、高级汉语水平的学习者作为课内泛读教材或课外阅读材料。内容可根据学习者的兴趣灵活选择搭配。

主要内容

本套丛书共分 10 册，每册含一个文化专题，每个专题配有 10 个故事，每个故事约 1000~1200 个汉字，以介绍中国文化知识为目的，以提高学习者中文阅读能力为目标，内容涉及中国历史、地理、民俗、神话、文化、艺术、汉语、传统节日、文学、古今名人轶事等方方面面。

每个故事均以导读问题开始，如"中国武术有什么特点""练习武术有什么意义和好处""'武术'的'武'字有什么含义"等。

每个故事配有与内容相关的图片。生词随课文同现，方便学习和阅读。练习包括阅读理解、语句练习、词汇练习、语法练习和写作练习。

主要特点

◻ 集知识性、趣味性、实用性为一体。

◻ 每课内容前后衔接而又相互独立。重复出现的生词每课都进行标注，学习者随便翻开哪一课都可以直接阅读。

◻ 课后练习与新 HSK 的测试形式相结合。

◎ 每个专题都自成体系，学习者可以根据自己的需要或兴趣，选择某个专题中的若干课文进行学习。

◎ 图文并茂，每篇文章都配有与内容相关的图片。

借此机会，我们要感谢国家汉办 / 孔子学院总部对本套丛书编写的大力支持，并感谢为编写本套丛书提供和整理部分素材的老师们：陈苏蓉、冯凌、胡维佳、刘颖、钱景炜、吴瑶、吴莉、项莉、赵文娟。也感谢协助把中文课文翻译成英文的吴轶恩（Ian Wollman）。

刘美如　吕丽娜
2013 年秋于美国波特兰

A Guide to the Use of This Book

Compilation Ideas

▣ Combination of language teaching and culture teaching

This series aims not only at developing students' reading skills, but also at helping them gain a deeper understanding of Chinese culture and developing their international vision and cross-cultural communication skills.

▣ Adherence to the characteristics of compilation and development trend of Chinese reading textbooks in the United States and in other countries

Based on the compilation ideas of helping students understand "what" to read (the contents), "why" to read (the reasons) and "how" to read (the methods), this series attaches much importance to being informative, fun, practical and easy. Every story starts with some lead-in questions, which stimulate students' interest in reading, enhance the interaction, and make students think before reading the story.

▣ In accordance with the national standards and the guideline

In reference to the *Standards for Foreign Language Learning in the 21st Century* formulated by American Council on the Teaching of Foreign Languages (ACTFL), this book observes the Five Goals (Five C's), namely

Communication, Cultures, Connections, Comparisons and Communities. Upon using this series of textbooks, students will improve their communication skills in Chinese, getting thorough understanding and mastery of Chinese culture and connecting it to other disciplines. It also cultivates students' ability of comparing the characteristics of different languages and cultures and applying it to their daily life and study.

In terms of the vocabulary, the series has revised its language data to control its degree of difficulty based on the *Chinese Proficiency Test Syllabus* and *The Graded Chinese Syllables, Characters and Words for the Application of Teaching Chinese to the Speakers of Other Languages* issued by Hanban of China.

The purpose of "learning reading through reading"

As for the design of exercises, this series, with equal emphasis on and appropriate proportion of the exercises of comprehension of the language and the texts, avoids too many exercises on grammar and semantics, striving to achieve the purpose of "learning reading through reading" while ensuring its interestingness.

Target Readers

Targeted at learners of Chinese language at intermediate or advanced level, it is used as an extensive reading textbook inside and outside the classroom. Students can choose what to learn according to their interests.

Contents

There are altogether 10 volumes in the series of *Stories from China*, each with a topic about culture. Each topic is provided with 10 stories. With approximate 1000–1200 Chinese characters, each story aims at introducing Chinese culture and improving students' reading ability in Chinese, encompassing Chinese history, geography, folk customs, legends, culture, arts, language, traditional festivals, literature, anecdotes of celebrities in ancient and contemporary times and other aspects.

Each story starts with some lead-in questions, such as "What features do Chinese martial arts have?", "What is the meaning of practicing martial arts, and what benefits can we get from it?", and "What's the meaning of *wu* in *wushu* (martial arts)?"

Pertinent pictures are provided for each story. New words are presented together with the text to facilitate students' learning and reading. Exercises are composed of the following parts: Reading Comprehension, Sentence-Matching Exercises, Vocabulary Exercises, Grammar Exercises, and Writing Practice.

Features

- Integrating informativeness with interestingness and practicalness.
- Each text is both connected with each other and independent from each other. With the new words repeatedly marked and explained in each lesson, students can understand them in any lesson they read.
- Exercises after each lesson are integrated with the questions in the new HSK test.

- Each topic is independent from each other. Therefore, students are free to choose a text under a certain topic based on their need or interest.
- Each story is provided with content-based pictures.

Acknowledgements

We would like to take this opportunity to thank Hanban/the Confucius Institute Headquarters for its support in the writing of this book series, and those who helped with information collecting and sorting. They are as follows: Chen Surong, Feng Ling, Hu Weijia, Liu Ying, Qian Jingwei, Wu Yao, Wu Li, Xiang Li and Zhao Wenjuan. We would also like to thank Ian Wollman for his help with the translation of the texts into English.

Meiru LIU & Lina LU

Autumn 2013 in Portland of the United States of America

中国历史年代简表
A Brief Chinese Chronology

Xiàcháo **夏朝**	**Xia Dynasty**	Around 2070 BC–1600 BC
Shāngcháo **商朝**	**Shang Dynasty**	1600 BC–1046 BC
Xī Zhōu **西周**	**Western Zhou Dynasty**	1046 BC–771 BC
Dōng Zhōu **东周**	**Eastern Zhou Dynasty** 770 BC–256 BC	Chūnqiū **春秋** **Spring and Autumn Period** 770 BC–476 BC
		Zhànguó **战国** **Warring States Period** 475 BC–221 BC
Qíncháo **秦朝**	**Qin Dynasty**	221 BC–206 BC
Hàncháo **汉朝**	**Han Dynasty** 206 BC–220 AD	Xī Hàn **西汉** **Western Han Dynasty** 206 BC–25 AD
		Dōng Hàn **东汉** **Eastern Han Dynasty** 25 AD–220 AD
Sānguó **三国**	**Period of the Three Kingdoms** 220 AD–280 AD	Wèiguó **魏国** **Kingdom of Wei** 220 AD–265 AD
		Shǔguó **蜀国** **Kingdom of Shu** 221 AD–263 AD
		Wúguó **吴国** **Kingdom of Wu** 222 AD–280 AD

Jìncháo **晋朝**	**Jin Dynasty** 265 AD–420 AD	Xī Jìn **西晋 Western Jin Dynasty** 265 AD–317 AD	
		Dōng Jìn **东晋 Eastern Jin Dynasty** 317 AD–420 AD	
Nán-Běi cháo **南北朝**	**Northern and Southern Dynasties** 420 AD–589 AD		
Suícháo **隋朝**	**Sui Dynasty** 581 AD–618 AD		
Tángcháo **唐朝**	**Tang Dynasty** 618 AD–907 AD		
Wǔdài **五代**	**Five Dynasties** 907 AD–960 AD		
Sòngcháo **宋朝**	**Song Dynasty** 960 AD–1279 AD	Běi Sòng **北宋**	**Northern Song Dynasty** 960 AD–1127 AD
		Nán Sòng **南宋**	**Southern Song Dynasty** 1127 AD–1279 AD
Yuáncháo **元朝**	**Yuan Dynasty** 1206 AD–1368 AD		
Míngcháo **明朝**	**Ming Dynasty** 1368 AD–1644 AD		
Qīngcháo **清朝**	**Qing Dynasty** 1616 AD–1911 AD		

目录

中国的朝代

cháodài,
dynasty

中国历史上著名的皇帝

导读问题　Lead-in Questions

1. 上图中的几个皇帝（huángdì, emperor）你听说过吗？你知道他们都是哪个朝代的吗？
2. 春秋战国时期，中国出现了哪些大思想家？
3. 三国鼎立（dǐnglì, to stand like a tripod）时期，中国出现了哪些大军事家（jūnshìjiā, militarist）？
4. 为什么说唐朝是中国最繁荣（fánróng, prosperous）的历史时期？
5. 哪个朝代是中国最后一个封建（fēngjiàn, feudal）王朝？

禹　Yǔ
a legendary ruler of the Xia
Tribe in history

治理　zhìlǐ
to govern, to manage

当时　dāngshí
at that time

部落　bùluò　tribe

首领　shǒulǐng
chief, leader, head

启　Qǐ　Yu's son

奴隶制　núlìzhì
slavery

公元　gōngyuán
Christian era

世袭制　shìxízhì
the hereditary system

甲骨文　jiǎgǔwén
oracle bone script

养蚕业　yǎngcányè
silkworm-raising industry

丝绸　sīchóu　silk

老子　Lǎozǐ　Lao Zi,
an ancient Chinese
philosopher

孔子　Kǒngzǐ　Confucius

孟子　Mèngzǐ
Mencius, an ancient Chinese
philosopher

中国有 5000 多年的文明史，是世界四大文明古国之一。

4000 多年前，有一个叫禹的人，因为成功治理洪水，成了当时夏部落的首领，他的儿子启建立了中国第一个奴隶制朝代——夏朝（约公元前 2070 年~公元前 1600 年）。世袭制就是从夏朝开始的，中国的传统历法——夏历①，也是夏朝就有的。

夏朝之后是商朝（公元前 1600 年~公元前 1046 年），甲骨文②就是在商朝开始使用的。商朝的青铜制造水平已经很高。夏商时期，中国已经出现了养蚕业和丝绸。

甲骨文

商朝之后是西周（公元前 1046 年~公元前 771 年）和东周（公元前 770 年~公元前 256 年）。东周分为春秋（公元前 770 年~公元前 476 年）和战国（公元前 475 年~公元前 221 年）两个时期。东周时期思想和文化发展很快，出现了老子、孔子、孟子等大思想家，以及伟

China, with over 5,000 years of history, is one of the four cradles of civilization.

Over 4,000 years ago, a man named Yu controlled the flood and became the ruler of the Xia Tribe. Qi, his son, established the Xia Dynasty (around 2070 BC-1600 BC), the first slavery dynasty in Chinese history. The Xia Dynasty marked the start of the hereditary system and the origination of China's traditional calendar, the Xia Calendar (also known as the lunar calendar).

The Shang Dynasty (around 1600 BC -1046 BC), succeeding the Xia Dynasty, witnessed the creation of the oracle bone scripts. The craftsmanship of bronze casting advanced in the Shang Dynasty. The Xia and Shang dynasties also marked the appearance of silkworm-raising industry and silk in China.

甲骨文

Succeeding the Shang Dynasty came the Western Zhou Dynasty (1046 BC-771 BC) and the Eastern Zhou Dynasty (770 BC-256 BC). Divided into the Spring and Autumn Period (770 BC-476 BC) and the Warring States Period (475 BC-221 BC), the Eastern Zhou Dynasty marked the rapid ideological and cultural advances and the appearance of great thinkers such as Lao Zi, Confucius, Mencius and

孔子

诗人　　shīrén　poet

屈原　　Qū Yuán
an ancient Chinese poet

孙子　　Sūnzǐ
Sun-tzu, an ancient Chinese
militarist

扁鹊　　Biǎnquè
an ancient Chinese medical
practitioner

战争　　zhànzhēng
war, battle

秦始皇　Qín Shǐhuáng
the First Qin Emperor

统一　　tǒngyī
to unify

货币　　huòbì
money, currency

修建　　xiūjiàn
to build, to construct

连接　　liánjiē
to connect

刘邦　　Liú Bāng
the founder of the Han
Dynasty

汉武帝　Hàn Wǔdì
Emperor Wu of the Han
Dynasty

才华　　cáihuá　talent

延续　　yánxù
to continue, to last

中国人端午节吃粽子，
就是为了纪念屈原

大的诗人屈原、军事家孙子、名医扁鹊。但是，春秋战国时期战争不断。

公元前 221 年，秦始皇统一中国，建立了封建王朝——秦朝（公元前 221 年~公元前 206 年）。这个时期中国有了统一的文字、货币。秦始皇还把春秋战国时期修建的长城连接起来，建成了万里长城。公元前 206 年，秦朝灭亡。

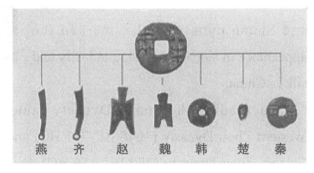

燕　齐　赵　魏　韩　楚　秦

秦始皇统一了货币

公元前 206 年，刘邦建立了汉朝（公元前 206 年~公元 220 年）。汉武帝刘彻是很有才华的皇帝。汉朝成为中国第一个非常强大的朝代，延续了 400 多年。这个时期的科技与文化非常繁荣。

poets like Qu Yuan, militarist Sun-tzu, famous medical practitioner Bian-que, etc. However, wars constantly broke out during the Spring and Autumn Period and the Warring States Period.

In 221 BC, the First Qin Emperor united China and established a feudal dynasty named Qin (221 BC–206 BC). He set up uniform systems of script and currency in China, and joined together the walls built during the Spring and Autumn Period and the Warring States Period to make the Great Wall of China. The Qin Dynasty fell in 206 BC.

写在竹简上的文字

The Han Dynasty (206 BC–220 AD) was founded by Liu Bang in 206 BC and lasted over 400 years. Emperor Wu of the Han Dynasty, named Liu Che, was an exceptionally talented emperor. The Han Dynasty was the first powerful dynasty in Chinese

万里长城

张骞　Zhāng Qiān
an imperial envoy of the Han Dynasty

出使　chūshǐ
to serve as an envoy abroad

西域　Xīyù
Western Region, today's Xinjiang Uygur Autonomous Region and the areas west to it

开通　kāitōng　to open up

丝绸之路　Sīchóu Zhī Lù
Silk Road, an ancient network of trade routes connecting the West with the East from China to the Mediterranean Sea

司马迁　Sīmǎ Qiān
a famous Chinese historian of the Han Dynasty

史记　Shǐjì
Shi Ji, or *Records of the Grand Historian*

造纸术　zàozhǐshù
paper-making craftsmanship

局面　júmiàn　situation

政治　zhèngzhì　politics

曹操　Cáo Cāo
a stateman and poet of the Period of the Three Kingdoms

诸葛亮　Zhūgě Liàng
the chancellor of Shu of the Period of the Three Kingdoms

汉朝分为西汉（公元前206年~公元25年）和东汉（公元25年~公元220年）。西汉时期张骞出使西域，开通

张骞雕像

了"丝绸之路"，司马迁完成了《史记》③。东汉时期出现了中国四大发明之一的造纸术。

《史记》

公元220年，东汉灭亡，出现了魏国、蜀国和吴国三国鼎立的局面，称为"三国时期"（公元220年~公元280年），中国又进入了长时间的战争。三国时期出现了很多著名的大政治家、大军事家，比如曹操、诸葛亮等。中国四大名

history and it grew very prosperous in science and culture. The Han Dynasty was divided into the Western Han Dynasty (206 BC-25 AD) and the Eastern Han Dynasty (25 AD-220 AD). In the Western Han Dynasty, Zhang Qian travelled to the Western Region (today's Xinjiang Uygur Autonomous Region and the areas west to it); the "Silk Road" trade network was

曹操雕像

opened up; and Sima Qian compiled *Shi Ji*, or *Records of the Grand Historian*. During the Eastern Han Dynasty, paper-making craftsmanship, one of the Four Great Inventions of China, had its first appearance.

After the Eastern Han Dynasty was decomposed in 220 AD, China broke up into three kingdoms—Kingdoms of Wei, Shu and Wu, and underwent a period of constant wars. This period is known as the Period of the Three Kingdoms (220 AD-280 AD). Many well-known statesmen and militarists such as Cao Cao and Zhuge Liang appeared in this period.

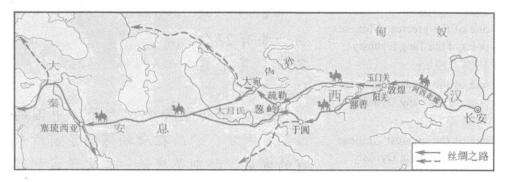

古代丝绸之路路线图

7

三国演义 Sānguó Yǎnyì

Romance of the Three Kingdoms

背景 bèijǐng background

分裂 fēnliè to split

开创 kāichuàng
to initiate

前所未有 qiánsuǒwèiyǒu
unprecedented

强盛 qiángshèng
powerful and prosperous

唐太宗 Táng Tàizōng
the second emperor of the
Tang Dynasty, i.e., Li Shimin

李世民 Lǐ Shìmín
the second emperor of the
Tang Dynasty

武则天 Wǔ Zétiān
an empress of the Tang Dynasty

诗歌 shīgē poem

书法 shūfǎ calligraphy

绘画 huìhuà to paint

李白 Lǐ Bái
one of the greatest Chinese
poets of the Tang Dynasty

杜甫 Dù Fǔ
one of the greatest Chinese
poets of the Tang Dynasty

白居易 Bái Jūyì
one of the greatest Chinese
poets of the Tang Dynasty

著④之一——《三国演义》就是以这段历史为背景写成的。

三国时期之后，中国又经历了西晋（公元265年~公元317年）、东晋（公元317年~公元420年）、南北朝（公元420年~公元589年）时期，经历了300多年的分裂和战争，直到隋朝（公元581年~公元618年）建立。虽然隋朝只有38年的历史，但是却统一了分裂多年的中国。隋朝在政治、经济、文化等方面发展很快，为唐朝（公元618年~公元907年）的繁荣打下了基础。

隋朝和唐朝是中国最繁荣的历史时期。唐朝持续了290年，开创了中国前所未有的强盛时代。唐朝一共有22位皇帝，其中包括著名的唐太

武则天画像

宗李世民和女皇帝武则天等。中国的诗歌、书法、绘画在唐朝得到了前所未有的发展，特别是唐诗，其文学成就最高，出现了李白、杜甫和白居易等大诗

Romance of the Three Kingdoms, one of the Four Masterpieces in Chinese literature, was written based on the history of this period.

After the Period of the Three Kingdoms, China got into splits and wars over 300 years, lasting from the Western Jin Dynasty (265 AD–317 AD), the Eastern Jin Dynasty (317 AD–420 AD), to the Southern and Northern Dynasties (420 AD–589 AD). China finally achieved its unification in the Sui Dynasty

纪念三国人物的三义庙，位于中国成都

(581 AD–618 AD). Although the Sui Dynasty had only 38 years of history, it made rapid advances in politics, economy and culture, laying a foundation for the prosperity of the Tang Dynasty (618 AD–907 AD).

The Sui and Tang dynasties were golden ages in Chinese history. The Tang Dynasty, an unprecedentedly glorious era lasting 290 years, was ruled by altogether 22 emperors, including the famous Emperor Tang Taizong, named Li Shimin, and the Empress Wu Zetian. Unprecedentedly rapid progress was made during the Tang Dynasty in Chinese poetry, calligraphy and painting. With the emergence of eminent poets such as Li Bai,

四川成都的杜甫草堂是杜甫曾经居住过的地方

海外　hǎiwài
overseas

火药　huǒyào
gunpowder

指南针　zhǐnánzhēn
compass

活字印刷术
huózì yìnshuāshù
moveable-type printing

少数民族　shǎoshù mínzú
minority ethnic group

政权　zhèngquán
regime

成吉思汗　Chéngjísī Hán
Genghis Khan

蒙古族　Měnggǔzú
Mongolian ethnic group

军事　jūnshì　military

控制　kòngzhì　to control

西亚　Xīyà　West Asia

国土　guótǔ
territory

马可·波罗　Mǎkě Bōluó
Marco Polo, a famous Italian traveler

人。当时的中国在世界上的地位也非常重要，现在生活在海外的华人也被称为"唐人"，就是这个原因。

唐代之后中国又出现了五代十国（公元907年～公元960年）的分裂局面。后来宋朝（公元960年～公元1279年）统一了中国，社会经济得到了很大发展，中国四大发明中的火药、指南针和活字印刷术就是在宋朝开始出现和使用的。

元朝（公元1206年～公元1368年）是中国历史上第一个由少数民族在全国范围内建立政权的朝代。当时在成吉思汗的领导下，蒙古族依靠强大的军事力量，控制了整个西亚地区，建立了中国有史以来国土面积最大的王朝。意大利商人马可·波罗就是在元朝时来到中国

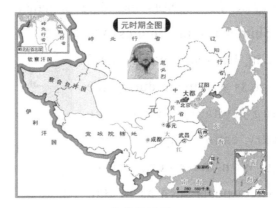

元朝疆域图

Du Fu and Bai Juyi, Tang Poetry achieved the greatest literary success. China at that time also took an important position in the world. As a result, Chinese in other countries now are still also referred to as the "Tang People".

China was split again in the Period of Five Dynasties and Ten Nations (907 AD–960 AD) following the Tang Dynasty. Later, in the Song Dynasty (960 AD–1279 AD), China was united and had a rapid social and economic growth. Three of the Four Great Inventions of China, namely gunpowder, compass and movable-type printing, were invented and used starting from the Song Dynasty.

The Yuan Dynasty (1206 AD–1368 AD) was the first dynasty in Chinese history established across the country by a minority ethnic group. Mongols, led by Genghis Khan, used their mighty military power and took control of the entire

指南针的前身——司南

West Asia, establishing a kingdom with the largest territory in Chinese history. Marco Polo, an Italian merchant who came to China in the Yuan Dynasty, gave a detailed account of its prosperity in his book *The*

中国的四大发明

详细	xiángxì	
detailed		
记载	jìzǎi	
to record		
景象	jǐngxiàng	
scene		
航海家	hánghǎijiā	
navigator		
郑和	Zhèng Hé	
an explorer, navigator and diplomat of the Ming Dynasty		
率领	shuàilǐng	to lead
西洋	Xīyáng	
West Ocean, referring to the present-day Southeast Asia, South Asia, the Middle East, Somalia and the Swahili Coast		
非洲	Fēizhōu	Africa
满族	Mǎnzú	
Manchu ethnic group		
康熙	Kāngxī	
an emperor of the Qing Dynasty		
乾隆	Qiánlóng	
an emperor of the Qing Dynasty		
雍正	Yōngzhèng	
an emperor of the Qing Dynasty		
盛世	shèngshì	
golden age, age of prosperity		

的。在根据他的经历写成的《马可·波罗游记》中，详细记载了当时元朝的繁荣景象。

明朝（公元 1368 年~公元 1644 年）是元朝之后另一个统一的朝代。这个时期著名的航海家郑和曾率领船队七次下西洋。他和他的船队最远曾到达现在的非洲。

清朝（公元 1616 年~公元 1911 年）是中国最后一个封建王朝，是 1616 年由满族建立的。在清朝的 12 位皇帝中，康熙和乾隆是最有名的两位皇帝。特别是乾隆，他在康熙、雍正两朝的基础上，进一步完成了多民族国家的统

康熙皇帝画像

一，使社会经济文化有了进一步发展，形成了中国历史上著名的"康乾盛世"。

Travels of Marco Polo.

The Ming Dynasty (1368 AD–1644 AD), a unified dynasty following the Yuan Dynasty, has a famous navigator named Zheng He (also known as Cheng Ho) who made seven western maritime expeditions with his sailing team and reached as far west as the present-day Africa.

郑和下西洋纪念邮票

The Qing Dynasty (1616 AD–1911 AD), established by the Manchu people in 1616, was the last feudal dynasty in Chinese history. Of its 12 emperors, Kangxi and Qianlong were the most famous. Qianlong, in particular, made further steps towards unifying the multinational states and developing its society, economy and culture on the basis of the two preceding periods of Kangxi and Yongzheng. During the reign of Kangxi and Qianlong, China enjoyed prosperity and was well-known as "High Qing" in Chinese history.

明朝、清朝的皇宫——故宫

文化注释

① 夏历

夏历是中国传统历法之一，也称为农历、阴历、古历、旧历等，中国的春节、中秋节等传统节日就是依照农历的日期制定的。

② 甲骨文

甲骨文是中国已发现的古代文字中时代最早、体系较为完整、刻在龟甲和兽骨上的文字。

③《史记》

《史记》是由司马迁编写的，记录了中国汉代以前3000多年的历史，包括政治、经济、文化等各方面的内容。

④ 四大名著

中国的四大名著是《三国演义》《水浒传》《西游记》《红楼梦》。

◇ 练习 ◇

一 阅读理解 Reading Comprehension

练习1：判断正误 True（√）or false（×）

例 老子、孔子、孟子是唐朝的大思想家。（ × ）

1. 中国的第一个朝代是公元前5000多年建立的。（　　）

2. 长城是秦朝的时候修建的。（　　）

3. 丝绸之路是在春秋战国时期开通的。（　　）

4. 三国时期出现了很多著名的文学家。（　　）

5. 唐朝开创了中国前所未有的强盛时代。（　　）

6. 中国的诗歌在唐朝得到了前所未有的发展。（　　）

7. 中国的四大发明是：火药、指南针、活字印刷术和造纸术。（　　）

8. 元朝是中国历史上最后一个由少数民族建立政权的朝代。（　　）

9. 意大利商人马可·波罗是汉朝时来到中国的。（　　）

10. 清朝是由蒙古族建立的。（　　）

练习2：选择正确答案 Choose the right answer

例 夏商时期，中国已经出现了＿＿＿A＿＿＿。

　　A. 丝绸　　　　　B. 造纸术　　　　C. 长城　　　　　D. 印刷术

1. 甲骨文是在夏朝之后的 ＿＿＿＿＿ 开始使用的。

　　A. 商朝　　　　　B. 隋朝　　　　　C. 宋朝　　　　　D. 战国时期

2. 春秋战国时期思想和文化发展很快，出现了＿＿＿＿＿等大思想家。

　　A. 张衡　　　　　B. 孔子　　　　　C. 屈原　　　　　D. 曹操

3. 李白、杜甫和白居易是唐朝时期的 ＿＿＿＿＿。

　　A. 大诗人　　　　B. 大军事家　　　C. 大思想家　　　D. 大艺术家

4. ＿＿＿＿＿开创了中国前所未有的强盛时代。

　　A. 元朝　　　　　B. 秦始皇　　　　C. 唐朝　　　　　D. 清朝

5. 唐朝一共有＿＿＿＿＿位皇帝。

　　A. 32　　　　　　B. 290　　　　　　C. 22　　　　　　D. 38

6. 中国处在分裂局面的朝代是＿＿＿＿＿。

　　A. 五代十国　　　B. 西汉　　　　　C. 元朝　　　　　D. 清朝

7. 元朝是中国有史以来 _____ 的王朝。

　　A. 人口最多　　　　B. 第一个统一　　C. 基础最好　　　　D. 国土面积最大

8. 《马可·波罗游记》详细记载了当时元朝的 _____ 。

　　A. 发明　　　　　　B. 繁荣景象　　　C. 世袭制　　　　　D. 甲骨文

9. 在清朝的皇帝中，康熙和 _____ 是最有名的两位皇帝。

　　A. 雍正　　　　　　B. 乾隆　　　　　C. 成吉思汗　　　　D. 武则天

10. 著名航海家郑和曾 _____ 他的船队七次下西洋。

　　A. 开创　　　　　　B. 控制　　　　　C. 率领　　　　　　D. 记载

语句练习 Sentence-Matching Exercises

连线　**Match the left side with the information on the right**

1. 郑和的船队最远到达的地方是　　　A. 是以三国鼎立的局面为背景写成的

2. 唐朝持续了 290 年　　　　　　　　B. 控制了整个西亚地区

3. 隋朝只有 38 年历史　　　　　　　 C. 当时元朝的繁荣景象

4. 中国的四大发明　　　　　　　　　D. 现在的非洲

5. 清朝是　　　　　　　　　　　　　E. 建立了中国第一个朝代——夏朝

6. 《马可·波罗游记》详细记载了　　 F. 是唐朝著名的女皇帝

7. 蒙古族依靠强大的军事力量　　　　G. 中国最后一个封建王朝

8. 武则天　　　　　　　　　　　　　H. 大部分是在宋朝开始出现和使用的

9. 《三国演义》　　　　　　　　　　 I. 却为后来唐朝的繁荣打下了基础

10. 禹的儿子　　　　　　　　　　　　J. 开创了中国前所未有的强盛时代

三 词汇练习 Vocabulary Exercises

用课文中学过的词语填空 **Fill in the blanks with words/expressions in this lesson**

强盛	率领	满族	延续	蒙古族
国土	统一	鼎立	朝代	《三国演义》

　　中国历史上的第一个　<u>朝代</u>　是夏朝。公元前 221 年，秦始皇_____中国，建成了万里长城。汉朝是中国第一个非常强大的朝代，_____了 400多年。在魏国、蜀国和吴国三国_____时期，中国又进入了长时间的战争，_____就是以这段历史为背景写成的。唐朝开始于公元 618 年，开创了中国前所未有的_____时代。当时的中国在世界上的地位非常重要。现在生活在海外的华人被称为"唐人"，就是这个原因。元朝是中国历史上第一个由少数民族在全国范围内建立政权的朝代，_____依靠强大的军事力量，建立了中国有史以来_____面积最大的王朝。明朝时期，著名的航海家郑和曾_____船队七次下西洋。清朝是中国最后一个朝代，是 1616 年由_____建立的。在清朝的 12 位皇帝中，康熙和乾隆是最有名的两位皇帝。

四 语法练习 Grammar Exercises

用所给的词语组句 **Make sentences with the words and phrases given**

例　前所未有的　唐朝　强盛时代　中国　开创了
　　<u>唐朝开创了中国前所未有的强盛时代。</u>

1. 长城　连接了　修建的　春秋战国时期　秦始皇　起来　把

_____

2.在唐朝　中国的　发展　诗歌、书法、绘画　前所未有的　得到了

_____

3.地位　唐朝时期　重要　中国　在世界上的　非常

_____

4.海外　的　生活在　现在　华人　这个原因　被称为　就是　"唐人"

_____

5.下西洋　航海家　明朝时期　著名的　郑和　曾　率领　船队　七次

_____

五 写作练习 Writing Practice

用下列词语造句 **Make sentences using the following words/phrases/structures**

1.……是……之一：_____

2. 出现了……的局面：_____

3. 为……打下了基础：_____

4. 前所未有：_____

5. 得到了……的发展：_____

6. ……，就是这个原因：_____

7. 被称为……：_____

8. 在……的领导下：_____

9. 特别是：_____

10. 进一步：_____

秦始皇统一中国

> Qín Shǐhuáng,
> the First Qin Emperor
>
> tǒngyī,
> to unify

2

荆轲刺秦王

导读问题　Lead-in Questions

1. 猜一猜，图中的人为什么想杀秦王？

2. 谁是中国的第一个皇帝（huángdì, emperor）？他的贡献（gòngxiàn, contribution）是什么？

3. 为什么说秦始皇统一并简化（jiǎnhuà, to simplify）文字是中华文化统一的基础？

4. 秦始皇为什么要烧掉关于"百家言论（bǎijiā yánlùn, views of different schools of thought）"的书？他为什么活埋（huómái, to bury alive）读书人？

5. 秦朝最后是怎么灭亡的？

公元　gōngyuán
Christian era

诸侯国　zhūhóuguó
different vassal states

秦国　Qínguó
State of Qin

打败　dǎbài　to defeat

嬴政　Yíng Zhèng
name of the First Qin
Emperor

世世代代　shìshìdàidài
from one generation to
another

延续　yánxù
to continue, to last

称号　chēnghào　title

始　shǐ　the first

世　shì　generation

治理　zhìlǐ
to govern, to manage,
to subdue

郡　jùn　prefecture

县　xiàn　county

官员　guānyuán　official

任命　rènmìng　to appoint

服从　fúcóng　to obey

命令　mìnglìng　to order

当时　dāngshí
at that time

权力　quánlì　power

公元前221年以前，也就是2200多年前，中国主要由七个诸侯国组成。后来秦国先后打败了其他六国，统一了中国，建立了秦朝，使中国变成了一个统一的大国。秦朝的国王嬴政觉得自己的功劳比以前任何一个国王都要大，而且认为他建立的秦朝会世世代代延续下去，就决定采用"皇帝"的称号，称自己为"始皇帝"。于是，他就成了中国历史上第一个皇帝——秦始皇。他希望他的后代会成为皇帝二世、三世……一直传到千世万世。

全国虽然统一了，可是怎样来治理这么大的一个国家呢？秦始皇决定先把全国分为三十六个郡，郡下面再分县。各级官员都由皇帝任命，都要服从皇帝的命令。国家的事情，无论大小，都由皇帝一个人决定。从这里我们可以看出，当时皇帝的权力有多大啊！

秦半两钱

秦量

秦衡

秦朝的钱币及测量重量和体积的工具

China was composed of seven major states before 221 BC, or over 2,200 years ago. After wiping out the other six states one after another, the State of Qin took control of China and founded the Qin Dynasty, making China a large unified country. Considering his achievement to surpass any other kings and believing the dynasty he set up would last forever, Yingzheng, the ruler of Qin, assumed the title of "emperor" and proclaimed himself "Shihuangdi (the first emperor)". Yingzheng thus became the first emperor in Chinese history, hoping he could pass down the throne to his

秦始皇出征雕像

descendents from one generation to another.

Although the country was unified, a question as to how to govern it was put forward. The First Qin Emperor divided the state into 36 prefectures with counties under their jurisdiction. Officials of each level were appointed by him and must obey his orders. State affairs, no matter big or small, were solely determined by the emperor, from which can be seen his power and authority.

秦始皇接受朝拜的雕像

政治	zhèngzhì	
politics		
制度	zhìdù	
system		
后世	hòushì	
descendent		
轨道	guǐdào	track
车轮	chēlún	wheel
活跃	huóyuè	
active		
相互	xiānghù	
mutual		
流传	liúchuán	
to spread, to hand down		
深远	shēnyuǎn	
profound, far-reaching		
逐渐	zhújiàn	
gradually		
货币	huòbì	
money, currency		
度量衡	dùliànghéng	
measurement		
往来	wǎnglái	
to contact		
流通	liútōng	
to circulate		

秦始皇不仅建立了一套非常完整的政治制度，而且在经济和文化等方面做出了很多贡献，对后世影响很大。在秦始皇统一中国之前，各国之间都没有统一的制度。

拿交通来说，各地的车辆大小不一样，车的轨道也有宽有窄，很不方便。于是秦始皇就统一了车辆和轨道的标准，规定车辆上两个车轮间的距离一致，轨道也一样宽。这样，一辆车就可以在全国行驶，非常方便。

在秦始皇统一中国之前，各诸侯国使用的文字也很不统一。即使是一样的文字，也有好几种写法。于是秦始皇就统一并简化文字，使各地的文化交流活跃起来，相互之间的交往也方便多了。文字的统一成为中华民族统一的重要基础，对中华文化的流传产生了非常深远的影响。

随着各地的交流逐渐增多，商业也发达起来，但是原来各诸侯国的货币形状、大小都不相同，使用的度量衡①的标准也不一样。秦始皇规定全国上下使用统一的货币和度量衡，使商业往来和货币流通变得非常方便。

The First Qin Emperor, who not only established a set of comprehensive political systems, but also unified many things in terms of economy and culture, had a great influence on later generations as there was no such uniformity among the states before he unified China.

In terms of transportation, it had been extremely inconvenient because carriages in each area were different in size, and the carriageways were different in width. The First Qin Emperor standardized the distance between the two wheels and the width of the carriageways, thus making a carriage able to travel across the whole country easily.

今字	各国不同的文字				
	齐	楚	燕	三晋	秦
马					
安					
乘					

There had been no unitary scripts before the First Qin Emperor unified China; even the same script had had several ways of writing. The First Qin Emperor unified and simplified the scripts, which promoted cultural exchange and mutual contact. The unification of scripts also laid an important foundation for the unification of the Chinese nation, exerting a profound influence on disseminating and handing down the Chinese culture.

With the growing contacts among regions, commerce flourished. However, neither the shape, size of the currency, nor the measures and weights were the same. The First Qin Emperor standardized coinage, weights and measures, which made the business contact and currency circulation quite convenient.

匈奴	Xiōngnú	Huns
派	pài	
to send (someone on mission)		
大将	dàjiàng	general
内地	nèidì	inland
防御	fángyù	
to defend		
侵犯	qīnfàn	to invade
修筑	xiūzhù	to build
连接	liánjiē	to connect
举世闻名	jǔshì wénmíng	
world-famous		
安定	āndìng	
stable; to stabilize		
谈论	tánlùn	to talk about
威信	wēixìn	prestige
功过	gōngguò	
merits and demerits		
是非	shìfēi	
rights and wrongs		
暴政	bàozhèng	tyranny
陈胜	Chén Shèng	
name of a farmer uprising leader		
吴广	Wú Guǎng	
name of a farmer uprising leader		
战争	zhànzhēng	war, battle

正当秦始皇忙着治理国家的时候，北方的匈奴打了进来。秦始皇派了一名大将带领三十万人去抵抗，并很快占领了匈奴生活的地区，秦始皇还命令内地人迁到这里生活。为了防御北方匈奴的再次侵犯，秦始皇不仅把原来各国在北方修筑的长城连接起来，而且还新建了不少长城。这样，新旧长城就连接成了一条很长的长城，这就是举世闻名的万里长城。

中国统一后，虽然人民的生活安定了、商业发达了，但是，秦始皇却发现有一些读书人喜欢谈论国家大事，影响了他的威信。为了统一思想，他下令，除了医药、农业等方面的书以外，所有关于百家言论②的书籍，都得交出来烧掉。第二年，秦始皇知道在首都还有一些人仍然在背后议论他的功过是非，他非常生气，就下令把那些人抓起来，还把其中460多名读书人都活埋了。秦始皇的暴政让老百姓生活得很苦，加快了秦朝的灭亡。公元前209年，陈胜、吴广发动了反对秦朝的战争。公元前206年，秦朝灭亡。

While the emperor was engaged in handling state affairs, the Huns in northern area invaded. He sent a general leading 300,000 soldiers to fight against the invaders and took control in no time of the areas where the Huns lived. The

秦始皇修建长城防御外来侵犯

emperor also ordered his people living inland to migrate there. To protect the northern areas from further invasions by the Huns, the First Qin Emperor joined together the northern walls built by the former states and added a number of new ones, thus constructing a very long wall—the world-famous Great Wall.

After the unification of China, people had a stable life and business prospered. The emperor, however, found that some literati like commenting on state affairs, which affected his prestige. To make people think like one mind, the emperor ordered that all books of schools of thoughts be burned, excluding those on medicine and agriculture. In the second year, when he was told that some people were still talking about his merits and demerits in the capital, the emperor was so furious that he arrested those people and buried alive over 460 literati of them. The First Qin Emperor's tyranny caused untold sufferings to the people and sped the fall of his dynasty. In 209 BC, Chen Sheng and Wu Guang started the uprising against the Qin Dynasty. In 206 BC, the Qin Dynasty ended.

文化注释

① **度量衡**

　　在古代，"度"是计量长短的工具，"量"是计量容积的器皿，"衡"是计量重量的工具。

② **百家言论**

　　指春秋战国时期遗留下来的儒家、道家、法家等各种思想流派的学说。

◇ 练习 ◇

阅读理解 Reading Comprehension

练习 1：判断正误 True（ √ ）or false（ × ）

例　公元前 221 年以前，中国主要由七个诸侯国组成。（ √ ）

1. 秦始皇是中国历史上第一个皇帝。（　　）

2. 秦始皇规定把全国分为三十六个郡。（　　）

3. 秦朝的各级官员都由人民任命。（　　）

4. 在秦始皇的统治下，各级官员决定自己的政事。（　　）

5. 秦始皇把全部权力集中在他自己一个人身上。（　　）

6. 秦始皇以前，中国没有统一的车辆和轨道标准。（　　）

7. 统一文字对中华文化的流传产生了巨大影响。（　　）

8. 秦始皇以前，商业往来不方便是因为没有皇帝。（　　）

9. 秦始皇修建万里长城是为了防御北方匈奴的侵犯。（　　）

10. 为了使经济更加发达，秦始皇下令烧掉百家言论的书籍。（　　）

练习 2：选择正确答案 Choose the right answer

例 公元前 221 年以前，中国主要是由 ____C____ 组成的。

 A. 皇帝二世、三世   B. 六个国家

 C. 七个诸侯国   D. 三十六个郡

1. 中国历史上第一个封建王朝的皇帝是 _____ 。

 A. 皇秦始   B. 皇帝二世

 C. 秦始皇   D. 秦国

2. 为了治理这么大的一个国家，秦始皇建立了 _____ 。

 A. "皇帝" 的称号

 B. 各级官员的责任制

 C. 一套完整的政治制度

 D. 自己的功绩

3. 在秦朝，国家的事情，无论大小，都由 _____ 。

 A. 皇帝一个人决定

 B. 各级官员治理

 C. 三十六个郡决定

 D. 郡下面的县决定

4. 为了 _____ ，秦始皇统一了车辆和轨道的标准。

 A. 车道有宽有窄

 B. 一辆车可以通行全国

C. 车轮的轨道一样宽

D. 车辆上两个轮子一样

5. 秦始皇简化并统一了文字，_____。

A. 所以识字的人越来越多了

B. 使文字产生了好几种写法

C. 使相互之间的交往方便多了

D. 使文字传播到很远的地方

6. 使用统一的度量衡和货币，_____。

A. 使商业往来和货币流通变得非常方便

B. 使银行的管理也统一了

C. 使各国的买卖公平了

D. 使货币的种类减少了许多

7. 秦始皇把新旧长城连接起来是为了 _____。

A. 将内地人迁到黄河附近居住、生产

B. 防御北方匈奴的侵犯

C. 保护秦朝的世袭制

D. 统一原来的七个诸侯国

8. 为了统一思想，秦始皇下令 _____。

A. 读书人把书交出来

B. 把影响他威信的书藏起来

C. 烧掉医药、农业等书籍

D. 烧掉关于百家言论的书籍

9. 秦始皇下令 _____ 。

    A. 挖很多大坑

    B. 把议论他功过是非的人活埋了

    C. 把生气的人抓起来

    D. 读书人好好儿看书

10. _____ 加速了秦朝的灭亡。

    A. 修建长城

    B. 使用统一的文字

    C. 秦始皇的暴政

    D. 中央集权制度

语句练习 Sentence-Matching Exercises

连线 **Match the left side with the information on the right**

1. 秦国的国王觉得自己功绩很大	A. 秦始皇修建了万里长城
2. 国家的事情，无论大小	B. 并采用了比较简单的写法
3. 各地的车辆大小不一样	C. 加快了秦朝的灭亡
4. 车轮的轨道统一以后	D. 使商业往来和货币流通变方便了
5. 秦始皇规定了统一的文字	E. 就采用了"皇帝"的称号
6. 各国度量衡的标准不一样	F. 把关于百家言论的书籍烧掉
7. 为了防御北方匈奴的侵犯	G. 因此车道也有宽有窄，很不方便
8. 统一的度量衡和货币	H. 因此商业往来有困难
9. 为了统一思想，秦始皇下令	I. 一辆车就可以通行全国
10. 秦始皇的暴政	J. 都由皇帝一个人决定

三 词汇练习 Vocabulary Exercises

用课文中学过的词语填空 **Fill in the blanks with words/expressions in this lesson**

治理	郡	县	距离	轨道
货币	度量衡	匈奴	防御	侵犯

秦始皇在公元前221年统一了中国。这么大的国家，怎么 <u>治理</u> 才好呢？首先，他把全国分为三十六个_____，再把郡分成很多_____。但是各级官员都要绝对服从他的命令。秦始皇还规定了很多统一的制度。按照他的规定，各地车辆的车轮有统一的_____，这样，车轮间的_____相同，一辆车可以通行全国。为了让各地的商业往来没有困难，秦始皇又规定全国用统一的_____和_____。这些统一的制度使商业很快发达起来。但是，北方的_____不断_____内地。为了使人民的生产和生活安定，秦始皇决定把原来各国在北方的长城连接起来，连成一条举世闻名的万里长城，_____匈奴的侵犯。

四 语法练习 Grammar Exercises

用所给的词语组句 **Make sentences with the words given**

例 建立了 非常完整的 秦始皇 一套 政治制度
<u>秦始皇建立了一套非常完整的政治制度。</u>

1. 各级官员 服从 由皇帝 都要 皇帝的命令 都 任命

2. 中华文化的　非常　流传　对　产生了　影响　深远的　文字的统一

_____

3. 万里长城　长城　成了　新旧　举世闻名的　连接

_____

4. 治理国家　正当　匈奴　的时候　打了进来　北方的　秦始皇　忙着

_____

5. 发动了　陈胜、吴广　战争　秦朝的　反对

_____

五 写作练习 Writing Practice

用下列词语造句 **Make sentences using the following words/phrases/structures**

1. 由……组成：_____

2. 无论……都……：_____

3. 从……可以看出……：_____

4. 不仅……而且……：_____

5. 拿……来说：_____

6. 即使……也……：_____

7. 随着：_____

8. 正当……的时候： _____

9. 为了…… ： _____

10. 举世闻名： _____

兵马俑

bīngmǎyǒng,
terra cotta warriors

制作兵马俑

导读问题　Lead-in Questions

1. 上图中的人在制作什么？你见过这些东西吗？
2. 建造（jiànzào, to build, to construct）秦始皇陵（Qín Shǐhuáng Líng, the Mausoleum of the First Qin Emperor）用了多长时间？
3. 兵马俑是什么时候被发现的？又是怎样被发现的？
4. 秦始皇陵周围为什么埋（mái, to bury）了几千个兵马俑？
5. 为什么秦始皇兵马俑陪葬（péizàng, to be buried with the dead）坑（kēng, pit）被誉为（bèi yùwéi, to be praised as）世界最大的地下军事（jūnshì, military）博物馆？

秦始皇 Qín Shǐhuáng
the First Qin Emperor

皇帝 huángdì
emperor

统一 tǒngyī
to unify

宫殿 gōngdiàn
palace

陵墓 língmù
mausoleum

模仿 mófǎng
to imitate

当时 dāngshí
at that time

咸阳 Xiányáng
the capital of the Qin
Dynasty

布局 bùjú
layout

周长 zhōucháng
perimeter

工程 gōngchéng
project

想象 xiǎngxiàng
to imagine

士兵 shìbīng
soldier

陶俑 táoyǒng
terracotta figurine

守护 shǒuhù
to keep watch on

秦始皇是中国的第一个皇帝，他第一次统一了中国，建立了秦朝。他从13岁继承王位就开始建造一个地下宫殿，作为自己死后的陵墓。秦始皇为了死后的生活能跟他活着的时候一样好，就模仿当时首都咸阳的布局，使用了很多人力和财物，在西安附近用30余年的时间建造了这座地下宫殿——秦始皇陵。秦始皇陵原来高约120米，现在高约76米，内城周长约2.5公里，外城周长约6.3公里。墓内建有各种复杂的宫殿。工程之大，现代人很难想象。在秦始皇陵

的地下还埋有几千个跟真人差不多大小的士兵陶俑，以及他们的马俑和车俑，守护着秦始皇陵。这些陶俑就是陪葬的兵马俑，至今已经被埋到地下2000多年了。

The First Qin Emperor, also the first emperor of China, unified China for the first time and established the Qin Dynasty. He had begun to work on an underground palace as his final resting place since he was 13 years old when he succeeded the throne. To make sure his afterlife would be as good as his earthly life, the emperor, imitating the layout of the then capital Xianyang and using huge human and financial resources, took over 30 years to construct a palace below ground near Xi'an—the Mausoleum of the First Qin Emperor. The mausoleum, originally measuring 120 meters high and now 76 meters high, has a perimeter of around 2.5 kilometers inside the mausoleum and around 6.3 kilometers outside it. There are various complex palaces inside the mausoleum. This is a magnificent project almost unimaginable for people in modern times. There are thousands of terracotta figurines. The life-sized terracotta warriors, together with their horses and chariots, were buried underground for over 2,000 years, keeping watch on the mausoleum.

位于陕西西安的秦始皇兵马俑博物馆

偶然　ǒurán
accidentally

排列　páiliè
to arrange

平方米　píngfāngmǐ
square meter

发掘　fājué
to excavate

级别　jíbié
level, rank

将军　jiāngjūn
general

铠甲　kǎijiǎ
armour

做工　zuògōng
workmanship

精细　jīngxì
fine

工艺　gōngyì
craftmanship, workmanship

服饰　fúshì
attire and adornment

表情　biǎoqíng
facial expression

姿势　zīshì
posture

这些兵马俑被静静地埋在地下，没有人发现他们。直到 1974 年，当地的农民在田里干活的时候，才偶然发现了这些被埋在地下的陶俑。这些兵马俑都整齐地排列在位于秦始皇陵东边的大坑里。目前人们一共在三个大坑①中发现了兵马俑。这些大坑面积约两万多平方米，朝向东边，像"品"字的形状排列着。坑中发掘出了 700 多件陶俑、100 多辆战车、400 多匹陶马、10 万多件兵器。

兵俑身高在 1.75 到 1.85 米之间。从他们身上穿的衣服、头上戴的帽子以及脚上穿的鞋可以看出，兵俑主要分为四个级别，分别代表当时军队里不同级别的将军和士兵。大部分兵俑身上都穿着铠甲，虽然不同的级别穿的铠甲不一

样，但是做工都十分精细，跟真的铠甲一样。可见当时秦朝制作铠甲的工艺已经非常发达。他们不仅服饰不同，表情、姿势以及手里拿的武器也都不同。你可以看到有的面带微笑，有的

No one noticed these terracotta warriors and horses buried quietly underground until 1974 when some local farmers, while working in the fields, accidentally found them. The terracotta army, neatly arranged in altogether 3 big pits, was found in the east part of the First Qin Emperor Mausoleum. Distributed in a layout like the Chinese character "品" and facing east, these pits cover an area of over 20,000 square meters. Inside the pits, more than 700 terracotta warriors, 100 war chariots, 400 terracotta horses and 100,000 arms were excavated.

The terracotta warriors are 1.75 meters to 1.85 meters in height. Judging from their attires, hats and shoes, they are divided into four ranks, respectively representing the generals and soldiers of different ranks in the army. Most warriors wear armours. Although the armours are different corresponding to the ranks, they are finely made and look like the real ones, showing the highly developed armour-making technology at that time. The warriors are different not only in their attires, but also in their facial

蹲　dūn
to crouch, to squat

弓　gōng
bow

剑　jiàn
sword, sabre

出土　chū tǔ
to unearth

锋利　fēnglì
sharp

叫唤　jiàohuan
to whinny

栩栩如生　xǔxǔ rú shēng
lifelike

惊叹　jīngtàn
to marvel at

秦国　Qínguó
State of Qin

久远　jiǔyuǎn
long

惊讶　jīngyà
surprised

奇迹　qíjì
miracle

遗产　yíchǎn
heritage

名录　mínglù
list

很严肃；有的站着，有的半蹲着；有的骑着马，有的坐着车；有的手里拿着弓，有的手里拿着剑。坑内出土的剑等兵器，虽然被埋在地下 2000 多年了，但依然锋利。

马俑的样子也很生动。有的两只耳朵都立着，像是

随时准备出发；有的嘴微微张开，像是在叫唤；还有的嘴巴紧闭，安静地站在那里。无论是人还是马，个个都栩栩如生，令人惊叹。秦始皇兵马俑陪葬坑被誉为世界最大的地下军事博物馆。我们可以想象，当时统一中国的秦国军队是多么强大！

最初的兵马俑都是彩色的，可是因为历史久远，被挖出来的时候，环境发生了变化，兵马俑上的颜色很快就消失了。

兵马俑被发现之后，世界上很多人都觉得很惊讶，认为这是人类创造的一个奇迹。1987 年，秦始皇陵及兵马俑被列入《世界遗产名录》。

expressions, postures and the arms holding in their hands. Look! Some are smiling, others look solemn; some are standing, others are half-crouching; some are riding horses, others are sitting on chariots; some are holding bows, others are holding sabres in their hands. The sabres and other arms excavated from the pits, though having been buried underground for over 2,000 years, are still extremely sharp.

The terracotta horses also have vivid appearances. Some horses, with both ears standing upright, look as if they were setting off at any time; some have their mouths open as if they were whinnying; while others are standing there quietly with  their mouths closed. Both the people and the horses look lifelike and awe-inspiring. From these burial pits of the terracotta warriors and horses, which are reputed as the largest underground military museum in the world, we can imagine how powerful the army of the State of Qin was at that time!

The terracotta warriors and horses, deeply buried below the earth for so long, were all colorized in their original state. However, when they were dug out, as the environment changed, they quickly lost their colors.

The Terracotta Warriors and Horses are considered to be a miracle of human creation and have shocked many people around the world. In 1987, the Mausoleum of the First Qin Emperor and Terracotta Warriors and Horses were inscribed to the World Heritage List.

文化注释

❶ 三个大坑

　　兵马俑陈列在三个大坑里面，按照发掘时间的先后，分别编号为一号坑、二号坑、三号坑。俑坑中陶俑、陶马按古代军队的编队排列。一号坑内是由 6000 多件陶俑、陶马及 40 余辆战车组成的长方形军阵；二号坑为步兵曲尺形混合军阵，有陶俑 900 多件、战车 89 辆、驾车陶马 356 匹、鞍马 100 余匹；三号坑中有 68 件陶俑、4 匹陶马和 1 辆战车，是一、二号坑军团的统帅部。

◇ 练习 ◇

一 阅读理解 Reading Comprehension

练习 1：判断正误 True（√）or false（×）

例　在秦始皇陵周围的地下埋有几千个兵俑、马俑和车俑。（　√　）

1. 秦始皇陵是一座地下宫殿。（　　　）

2. 秦始皇陵现在高约 120 米。（　　　）

3. 陪葬的陶俑叫作兵马俑。（　　　）

4. 这些兵马俑被静静地埋在地下一个世纪。（　　　）

5. 2000 年，当地的农民偶然发现了埋在地下的兵马俑。（　　　）

6. 这些兵马俑都整齐地排列在秦始皇陵左右。（　　　）

7. 兵俑身上穿的衣服、头上戴的帽子都一样。（　　　）

8. 兵俑表情、姿势以及手里拿的武器都不相同。（　　　）

9. 马俑的样子个个都栩栩如生。（　　　）

10. 埋在地下的兵马俑是彩色的。（　　　）

练习 2：选择正确答案 Choose the right answer

例 秦始皇是中国的第一个皇帝，他建立了____A____。

　　A. 秦朝　　　　　B. 汉朝　　　　　C. 唐朝　　　　D. 明朝

1. 秦始皇 13 岁继承王位的时候就开始建造一个地下宫殿，作为_____。

　　A. 休假的宫殿　　　　　　　　B. 咸阳最美的建筑

　　C. 自己死后的陵墓　　　　　　D. 战争时使用

2. 建造这座地下宫殿用了_____的时间。

　　A. 十几年　　　B. 二十年　　　C. 十三年　　D. 三十多年

3. 这座地下宫殿后来被人们称为_____。

　　A. 秦始皇陵　　　B. 地下皇宫　　　C. 陵墓　　　D. 军事博物馆

4. 在秦始皇陵周围的地下还埋有_____。

　　A. 兵俑和车俑　　　　　　　　B. 马俑和车俑

　　C. 马俑和兵俑　　　　　　　　D. 兵俑、车俑和马俑

5. 这些兵马俑是用_____做成的。

　　A. 铜　　　　　B. 陶　　　　　C. 铁　　　　D. 瓷

6. 这些陪葬的兵马俑被埋在地下已经_____了。

　　A. 2001 年　　　B. 2000 多年　　　C. 201 年　　D. 1974 年

7. 兵俑身上穿的衣服代表着当时军队里_____。

　　A. 士兵来自不同的地方　　　　B. 不同种类的士兵

　　C. 制作铠甲的工艺非常发达　　D. 不同等级的将军和士兵

8. 秦始皇陵里的人和马，个个都_____。

    A. 很难想象   B. 嘴巴紧闭   C. 栩栩如生   D. 面带微笑

9. 秦始皇兵马俑陪葬坑被誉为_____。

    A. 世界最大的地下军事博物馆   B. 非常著名的陵墓

    C. 用时最长的地下宫殿   D. 世界上陪葬品最多的陵墓

10. 兵马俑被认为是_____，被列入《世界遗产名录》。

    A. 秦国军队强大无比   B. 人类创造的一个奇迹

    C. 当时秦朝制作铠甲的工艺非常发达   D. 工程的浩大很难想象

语句练习 Sentence-Matching Exercises

连线 Match the left side with the information on the right

1. 秦始皇建造了一个地下宫殿   A. 跟真人差不多大小

2. 当地的农民在田里干活的时候   B. 分别代表当时军队里不同的等级

3. 兵俑身上的铠甲   C. 作为自己死后的坟墓

4. 秦始皇陵的兵马俑   D. 秦始皇陵东边的大坑里

5. 秦始皇兵马俑陪葬坑被誉为   E. 陪葬的兵俑、车俑、马俑

6. 几千个兵俑的尺寸   F. 已经非常发达

7. 秦朝制作铠甲的工艺   G. 是用来陪葬的

8. 兵俑不仅服饰不同   H. 世界最大的地下军事博物馆

9. 兵马俑指的是   I. 而且表情、姿势也都不相同

10. 这些兵马俑都整齐地排列在   J. 才偶然发现了被埋在地下的陶俑

三 词汇练习 Vocabulary Exercises

用课文中学过的词语填空 **Fill in the blanks with words/expressions in this lesson**

精细	奇迹	宫殿	惊讶	铠甲
陵墓	模仿	栩栩如生	兵马俑	排列

秦始皇 __模仿__ 当时首都咸阳的布局建造了秦始皇陵。秦始皇陵是秦始皇为自己建造的_____，它的地下埋葬着几千个陪葬的_____，守护着秦始皇陵。这些兵马俑都整齐地_____在秦始皇陵东边的大坑里。大部分兵俑身上都穿着_____，虽然不一样，但都十分_____。马俑的样子也很生动。无论是人还是马，个个都_____，令人惊叹。秦始皇兵马俑陪葬坑被誉为世界上最大的地下军事博物馆。兵马俑被发现后，世界上很多人都觉得很_____，认为这是人类创造的一个_____。

四 语法练习 Grammar Exercises

用所给的词语组句 **Make sentences with the words and phrases given**

例 可以想象　当时的　强大　秦国军队　是　我们　多么
我们可以想象，当时的秦国军队是多么强大。

1. 建造　秦始皇　财物和人力　这座地下宫殿　使用了　很多

_____

2. 几千个　在秦始皇陵的地下　有　跟真人　大小　的　士兵陶俑　差不多

_____

3. 已经　2000 多年　了　至今　埋在　被　地下　这些兵马俑

_____

4. 士兵和将军　兵俑　当时　分为　军队里　代表　四个级别　不同级别的

_____

5. 虽然　但　被　埋在　2000 多年了　地下　锋利　依然　剑等兵器　出土的

_____

五 写作练习 Writing Practice

用下列词语造句　Make sentences using the following words/phrases/structures

1. 跟……一样：_____

2. 至今：_____

3. 直到……才……：_____

4. 从……可以看出：_____

5. 可见：_____

6. 有的…… 有的……还有的……：_____

7. 无论 ……还是……：_____

8. 栩栩如生：_____

9. 令人惊叹：_____

10. 被誉为……：_____

万里长城 4

孟姜女哭长城

导读问题　Lead-in Questions

1. 图中的女孩儿为什么哭？古时候没有机器设备，长城是怎么修建
   （xiūjiàn, to build, to construct）的？
2. 万里长城最早是什么时候开始修建的？
3. 为什么要修建长城？
4. 万里长城建在中国的什么地方？
5. 万里长城在中国历史上起到了什么样的作用？

建筑　jiànzhù
architectural work

起点　qǐdiǎn
starting point

河北省　Héběi Shěng
a province of China

山海关　Shānhǎi Guān
a mountain pass of the Great Wall

甘肃省　Gānsù Shěng
a province of China

嘉峪关　Jiāyù Guān
a mountain pass of the Great Wall

公元　gōngyuán
Christian era

防御　fángyù
to defend

侵犯　qīnfàn
to invade

朝代　cháodài
dynasty

皇帝　huángdì　emperor

屏障　píngzhàng
(protective) screen

秦始皇　Qín Shǐhuáng
the First Qin Emperor

统一　tǒngyī
to unify

连接　liánjiē
to connect

中国的万里长城非常有名，是世界上最长的建筑，也是人类历史上最伟大的建筑之一。它位于中国北部，起点是今天河北省的山海关，终点是甘肃省的嘉峪关，全长六千多公里，也就是一万二千多里，所以被称为"万里长城"。

长城不是一个时期修建成的。最早的长城在公元前 7 世纪的春秋战国时期就已经开始修建了①。为了防御来自北方的侵犯，中国古代多数朝代的皇帝都会花大量的金钱和人力去修建长城。两千多年以来，长城不断地被修建、加固，成为防御外来侵犯的一道屏障。秦始皇统一中国后修建并连接起来的长城叫作秦长城。后来又有了汉长城和明长城，也就是汉朝和明朝时期修建的长城。

长城修建在高山上，高 10 米左右。

The Great Wall of China is very famous. It is the longest architectural work in the world as well as one of the greatest architectal works in human history. Located in northern China with its starting point at today's Shanhaiguan in Hebei Province and end point at Jiayuguan in Gansu Province, it spans a total length of over 6,000 kilometers (or 12,000 *li*), so it is referred to as "the Great Wall of Ten Thousand Miles".

河北省的山海关

甘肃省的嘉峪关

The Great Wall wasn't built during just one period of time. The earliest construction of the Great Wall had already begun in the Spring and Autumn Period in 7th century BC. In order not to be invaded by people from northern China, emperors of many dynasties of ancient China spent enormous sums of money and human resources to build the Great Wall, which became a screen defending against alien invasion. The Great Wall built and connected after the First Qin Emperor united China was known as the Qin Great Wall. Afterwards, there were the Han Great Wall and the Ming Great Wall, namely the Great Wall built during the Han Dynasty and the Ming Dynasty.

Built on high mountains, the Great Wall is around ten meters in height. In ancient times, soldiers kept guard day and night on top of the Great Wall

古时候，长城上面日日夜夜都有士兵守卫，还有可以传递信号的烽火台，所以长城外面的敌人很难打进来。

北京附近的箭扣长城

长城是用石头和特别烧制的砖建造的，非常坚固。然而，修建长城却非常辛苦。古时候没有机器设备，几百斤重的大石头也只能靠人搬到山上。千百年来，为了修建长城而死去的老百姓不计其数，民间一直流传着"孟姜女哭长城"的故事：传说秦始皇时期有一个女人叫孟姜女，结婚不久，她丈夫就被抓去修建长城。孟姜女在家日夜等待，她的丈夫却一直没有回来。冬天到了，孟姜女去给丈夫送棉衣，她走了很多天才走到长城，却得知丈夫已经死了。孟姜女伤心地哭了几天几夜，最后把长城哭倒了。

日日夜夜　rìrìyèyè
every day and every night

士兵　shìbīng　soldier

守卫　shǒuwèi
to keep guard

传递　chuándì
to send, to transfer

烽火台　fēnghuǒtái
beacon tower

好汉碑

建造　jiànzào
to build, to construct

流传　liúchuán
to spread, to hand down

孟姜女　Mèngjiāngnǚ
a legendary character in a
Chinese folk story

棉衣　miányī
cotton-padded clothes

得知　dézhī
to know, to be told (about
something)

and the beacon towers were used to send signals, so it was very difficult for enemies outside the Great Wall to attack.

The Great Wall, made of stones and specially made bricks, was extremely sturdy. However, the construction of the Great Wall was toilsome, as there were no machines in ancient times, and stones weighing several hundred kilograms could only be carried uphill by people. Over a thousand years, countless people died from toil. Legend has it that there was a woman called Mengjiangnu in the reign of the First Qin Emperor, whose husband was

北京附近的金山岭长城

enlisted to build the Great Wall not long after they got married. Mengjiangnu waited at home day and night, but her husband never came back. When winter came, she went to give her husband some cotton-padded clothes. After walking for days, Mengjiangnu finally arrived at the Great Wall only to find that her husband had already died. After Mengjiangnu cried for days, the Great Wall finally crumbled to dust.

The Great Wall we see today was mostly built during the Ming Dynasty, and thus is known as the Ming Great Wall. Badaling, the best preserved section of the Great Wall built during the Ming Dynasty, was the closest to the city areas of Beijing and is one of the most famous tourist attractions in Beijing. Being the best place to admire the Great Wall and the section of

八达岭　Bādá Lǐng
a section of the Great Wall near Beijing

市区　shìqū
city area, urban district

观赏　guānshǎng　to view

慕田峪　Mùtián Yù
a section of the Great wall near Beijing

古北口　Gǔběikǒu
a section of the Great Wall near Beijing

司马台　Sīmǎtái
a section of the Great Wall near Beijing

金山岭　Jīnshān Lǐng
a section of the Great Wall near Chengde City, Hebei Province

天津　Tiānjīn
one of the four municipalities in China

黄崖关　Huángyá Guān
a mountain pass of the Great Wall

游览　yóulǎn
to tour, to travel

胜地　shèngdì　resort

雄伟　xióngwěi　majestic

壮观　zhuàngguān
spectacular

遗产　yíchǎn　heritage

名录　mínglù　list

勇往直前
yǒngwǎng-zhíqián
advance bravely

现在我们看到的长城基本上都是在明代修建的，称为明长城。明长城中保存得最好的是北京的八达岭长城，离北京市区最近，坐车大约一个多小时，是北京最有名的旅游景点之一，每天都有非常多的人去那里旅游，因为那里是观赏长城最好的地方之一。

北京附近的八达岭长城

除了八达岭长城以外，北京附近还有慕田峪长城、古北口长城、司马台长城和金山岭长城等。天津黄崖关长城、河北山海关、甘肃嘉峪关也是著名的长城游览胜地，也都非常雄伟壮观。

1987年，中国的长城被列入《世界遗产名录》。

在中国，我们常听人们说"不到长城非好汉"②，意思就是：不管有多少困难，我们一定要达到目的，这体现了一种不怕困难、勇往直前的精神。

the Great Wall closest to downtown Beijing, it takes travelers a little longer than an hour to get there by bus and attracts a large number of tourists every day. Aside from Badaling, the sections of the Great Wall at Mutianyu, Gubeikou,

北京附近的司马台长城

Simatai and Jinshanling in the vicinity of Beijing, Huangyaguan of Tianjin, Shanhaiguan of Hebei, and Jiayuguan of Gansu are also magnificent and spectacular and known as famous tourist resorts.

In 1987, the Great Wall of China was listed in the World Heritage List.

In China, it is often heard that, "He who has never been to the Great Wall is not a true man", meaning that a goal must be achieved in spite of whatever difficulties, reflecting the spirit of advancing bravely against all odds.

北京附近的慕田峪长城

文化注释

❶ 春秋战国时期的长城

春秋时期，诸侯国之间常有战争，最早在边界修建长城的是楚国（位于今天湖北省、河南省内）和齐国（位于今天的山东省内）。战国时期，北方一些诸侯国为防御外来侵犯修建了长城，包括燕长城、赵长城和秦长城。秦始皇时期的长城就是把北方的这些长城连接起来修建而成的。

❷ 不到长城非好汉

出自毛泽东的《清平乐·六盘山》，作于 1935 年 10 月，表现的是不达目的不罢休的决心。这句话的意思是：到了长城，不登到顶峰就不是英雄好汉。

◇ 练习 ◇

一 阅读理解 Reading Comprehension

练习 1：判断正误 True（√）or false（×）

例 万里长城是人类历史上最伟大的建筑之一。（ √ ）

1. 万里长城位于中国北部。（　　）

2. 万里长城全长一万公里。（　　）

3. 秦始皇统一中国后，把北方的长城连接了起来。（　　）

4. 汉长城和明长城是秦朝时期修建的长城。（　　）

5. 万里长城的修建，从战国到明朝，历经两千年。（　　）

6. 修建长城是为了防御外来侵犯。（　　　）

7. 长城是用石头和特别烧制的砖建造的，非常坚固。（　　　）

8. 现在我们看到的长城都是秦始皇在明代修建的。（　　　）

9. 明长城中保存得最好的是司马台长城。（　　　）

10. "不到长城非好汉"的意思是：中国人都去过长城。（　　　）

练习 2：选择正确答案 **Choose the right answer**

例 中国的万里长城非常有名，是世界上最长的＿＿＿A＿＿＿。

　　A. 建筑　　　　　B. 屏障　　　　　C. 烽火台　　　　D. 路程

1. 长城的起点是山海关，终点是＿＿＿＿＿＿＿＿。

　　A. 八达岭　　　B. 司马台　　　　C. 慕田峪　　　　D. 嘉峪关

2. 最早的长城在公元前 7 世纪的＿＿＿＿＿＿＿时期就已经开始修建了。

　　A. 秦朝　　　　B. 明朝　　　　　C. 春秋战国　　　D. 汉朝

3. 秦始皇统一中国后修建并连接起来的长城叫作＿＿＿＿＿＿＿。

　　A. 秦长城　　　B. 八达岭长城　　C. 烽火台　　　　D. 丝绸之路

4. 修建长城的目的是＿＿＿＿＿＿＿。

　　A. 防御来自北方的侵犯　　　　　B. 开发旅游景点

　　C. 传递信号　　　　　　　　　　D. 被列入《世界遗产名录》

5. 长城上的烽火台是用来＿＿＿＿＿＿＿的。

　　A. 加固长城　　　B. 防御　　　　C. 传递信号　　　D. 烧制砖头

6. 古时候没有机器设备，几百斤重的大石头也只能靠人＿＿＿＿＿＿＿。

　　A. 连接　　　　B. 防御　　　　　C. 烧制　　　　　D. 搬到山上

7. "孟姜女哭长城"的故事告诉我们：_____。

    A. 孟姜女写了这个故事   B. 修建长城而死去的老百姓不计其数

    C. 孟姜女防御外来侵犯   D. 加固长城很重要

8. 孟姜女结婚不久，_____。

    A. 冬天就到了   B. 伤心地哭了几天几夜

    C. 她丈夫就被抓去修建长城   D. 就去修建长城

9. 每天都有非常多的游人去八达岭长城旅游观光，因为那里_____。

    A. 可以看见孟姜女   B. 是观赏长城最好的地方

    C. 可以坐车去   D. 有烽火台

10. "不到长城非好汉"的意思是：_____。

    A. 不管有多少困难，一定要达到目的   B. 只有好汉才能到长城去

    C. 到长城的人不是好汉   D. 长城上有很多好汉

■ 语句练习 Sentence-Matching Exercises

连线 **Match the left side with the information on the right**

1. 中国最早的长城	A. 基本上都是在明代修建的
2. 秦始皇统一中国后	B. 不计其数
3. 万里长城全长六千多公里	C. 在公元前 7 世纪前后就开始修建了
4. 中国的 "万里长城"	D. 是观赏长城最好的地方之一
5. 我们今天看到的长城	E. 不管有多少困难，一定要达到目的
6. 修建长城的目的是	F. 靠人工搬到山上
7. 几百斤重的大石头只能	G. 防御来自北方的侵犯
8. 为了修建长城而死去的老百姓	H. 也就是一万二千多里，所以被称为 "万里长城"
9. 北京八达岭长城	I. 是世界上最长的建筑
10. "不到长城非好汉"的意思	J. 修建并连接起来的长城叫作秦长城

三 词汇练习 Vocabulary Exercises

用课文中学过的词语填空 **Fill in the blanks with words/expressions in this lesson**

建筑	烽火台	修建	不计其数	建造
坚固	辛苦	侵犯	屏障	防御

中国的"万里长城"是人类历史上最伟大的 <u>建筑</u> 之一。中国最早的长城在公元前 7 世纪就已经开始_____了。秦始皇统一中国后，把北方的长城连接了起来。中国古代多数朝代的皇帝都会花大量的金钱和人力修建长城，这是为了_____来自北方的_____。古时候，长城上面日日夜夜都有士兵守卫，还有可以传递信号的_____，所以长城外面的敌人很难打进来。两千多年来，长城不断地被修建、加固，成为防御外来侵犯的一道_____。长城是用石头和特别烧制的砖_____的，非常_____。然而，修建长城却非常_____。几百斤重的大石头只能靠人搬到山上。为了修建长城而死去的老百姓_____。

四 语法练习 Grammar Exercises

用所给的词语组句 **Make sentences with the words and phrases given**

例 之一 中国的 是 万里长城 人类历史上 建筑 最伟大的
　　<u>中国的万里长城是人类历史上最伟大的建筑之一。</u>

1. 位于 全长 中国北部 六千多公里 万里长城

_____

2. 为了 长城 修建 是 来自 北方的 防御 侵犯

_____

3. 上面　长城　日日夜夜　传递信号的　守卫　烽火台　都有　可以　还有　士兵

_____

4. 石头　长城　是……的　用　和　特别烧制的　建造　砖

_____

5. 孟姜女　没有回来　一直　可是　在家　等待　她的丈夫　日夜

_____

五 写作练习 Writing Practice

用下列词语造句 **Make sentences using the following words/phrases/structures**

1. 也就是：_____

2. 为了……：_____

3. 日日夜夜：_____

4. 然而：_____

5. 不计其数：_____

6. 流传：_____

7. 之一：_____

8. 除了……以外，还……：_____

9. 体现了：_____

10. 勇往直前：_____

大唐盛世

> shèngshì,
> prosperous age

唐代大诗人李白

1. 你知道唐诗《静夜思》吗？你猜上图中的人在想什么呢？

2. 你知道什么是唐三彩吗？

3. 为什么说唐朝在文学方面的成就是前所未有（qiánsuǒwèiyǒu, unprecedented）的？

4. 唐朝的文化和特产（tèchǎn, speciality, special product）沿着（yánzhe, along...）丝绸之路（Sīchóu Zhī Lù, Silk Road）传到了哪些国家？

5. 海外（hǎiwài, overseas）华人生活的地方为什么叫作"唐人街"？

唐朝（公元618年~公元907年）是中国历史上最强盛的时期之一。那时候的中国，社会安定，经济发达，国力强大，是亚洲的经济和文化中心，在世界上也有着十分重要的地位。直到现在，人们一提起唐朝，都会称赞它为"大唐盛世"。

唐朝的社会经济非常繁荣，它的繁荣程度超过了中国以前任何一个朝代，光是水利工程就有200多个，比它之前各个朝代修建的同类

唐三彩

工程的总和还要多。当时的手工业和工艺也很发达，不但品种多样，而且达到了世界领先水平。其中最著名的要数唐三彩。唐三彩是一种精美的陶器，有黄、绿、褐、蓝等多种颜色，形象生动，色彩鲜艳，在唐朝的时候就已经销售到世界各地，深受各国人民的喜爱。

公元　gōngyuán
Christian era

强盛　qiángshèng
powerful and prosperous

安定　āndìng　stable

国力　guólì　national power

当时　dāngshí　at that time

亚洲　Yàzhōu　Asia

提起　tíqǐ　to mention

称赞　chēngzàn
to praise, to commend

繁荣　fánróng
flourishing, prosperous

朝代　cháodài　dynasty

水利　shuǐlì
irrigation works

工程　gōngchéng
project

修建　xiūjiàn
to build, to construct

同类　tónglèi　similar kind

手工业　shǒugōngyè
handicraft industry

工艺　gōngyì
technology

品种　pǐnzhǒng
variety

陶器　táoqì
pottery

鲜艳　xiānyàn
bright, beautiful

The Tang Dynasty (618 AD-907 AD) was one of the most prosperous periods in Chinese history. Being the economic and cultural center in Asia and taking a significant position in the world, China at that time enjoyed stable society, developed economy, and influential national power. Even today, it is acclaimed as the "Gold Age of Tang."

唐三彩：骆驼上的乐队

The Tang Dynasty enjoyed social and economic prosperity, and it was more flourishing than any other preceding dynasties in China. Its irrigation works totaled over 200, surpassing the total number in the similar projects built in all dynasties before. The handicraft industry and technology of that time were also highly developed and diversified in variety, leading the way in the world. Among them, the Tang Trio-colored Glazed Pottery was the most famous. The Tang Trio-colored Glazed Pottery, with vivid images and bright and beautiful colors like yellow, green, brown and blue, was an exquisite pottery already sold around the world during the Tang Dynasty and much loved

唐三彩：侍女（唐代以胖为美）

长安　Cháng'ān
the capital of the Tang Dynasty, the present-day Xi'an

都市　dūshì
city, metropolis

罗马　Luómǎ　Rome

空前　kōngqián
unprecedented

诗歌　shīgē　poem

黄金时代　huángjīn shídài
golden age

记载　jìzǎi　to record

诗人　shīrén　poet

李白　Lǐ Bái
one of the greatest Chinese poets of the Tang Dynasty

杜甫　Dù Fǔ
one of the greatest Chinese poets of the Tang Dynasty

白居易　Bái Jūyì
one of the greatest Chinese poets of the Tang Dynasty

古体诗　gǔtǐshī
ancient-style poetry

固定　gùdìng
to fix

格律　gélǜ
meter, rules and forms of classical poetic composition

近体诗　jìntǐshī
"modern style" poem

由于经济发达，生活安定，这个时期，人口增长得也非常快。公元 8 世纪的时候，人口就已经超过了 5000 万，是当时世界上人口最多的国家之一。唐朝的首都是长安（今陕西省西安市），光这里的人口就已经超过了 100 万，是当时国际性的大都市，也是东方文明的中心，历史上有"西有罗马，东有长安"的说法，可见它有多么重要。

今天的西安古城墙

唐朝在文学和艺术方面的成就也是空前的。那是中国诗歌发展的黄金时代，有文字记载的唐诗就有近 5 万首，出自 2200 多位唐代诗人之手，其中最著名的诗人有李白、杜甫和白居易。唐诗成为最有代表性的中国古代诗歌，代表了中国古代诗歌的最高成就。唐代既有形式比较自由的古体诗，也有形式固定、讲究格律的近体诗①。近体诗从每句的字

by people in many countries.

The economic development and stable life boosted the rapid population growth in this period. With its population already surpassing 50 million in the 8th century, China became one of the most populous countries in the

西安古城门

world. Chang'an (the present-day Xi'an of Shaanxi Province), the capital of the Tang Dynasty with a population of over one million, was an international metropolis and also the center of Oriental civilization. A saying "Rome in the West, Chang'an in the East" showed how important it was.

Unprecedented achievements were also made in literature and art in the Tang Dynasty. Chinese poetry enjoyed golden age in this period. Written record showed that there were almost fifty thousand poems written by over 2,200 poets in the Tang Dynasty and the most famous poets were Li Bai, Du Fu, and Bai Juyi. Tang Poetry became the most representative of China's ancient poetry, showing the highest achievements of China's ancient poetry. In the Tang Dynasty, there were not only

成都杜甫草堂的杜甫雕像

classical poems with free forms, but also the "modern style" poems with

绝句　juéjù
quatrain

律诗　lǜshī
poem of eight lines, each
containing five or seven
characters with a strict tonal
pattern and rhyme scheme

排律　páilǜ
poem of more than ten lines,
long regulated verse (usu.
with each line containing
five or seven characters)

脍炙人口　kuàizhì-rénkǒu
popular

霜　shuāng
frost

举头　jǔ tóu
to raise one's head

雕塑　diāosù
sculpture

石雕　shídiāo
stone carving

泥塑　nísù
clay sculpture

雄伟　xióngwěi
majestic

做工　zuògōng
work

壮观　zhuàngguān
spectacular

佛像　fóxiàng
Buddha

李白雕像

数来看，可以分为五字一句的五言诗和七字一句的七言诗；从句数来看，主要可以分为四句一首的绝句、八句一首的律诗和十句以上的排律。李白的《静夜思》就是一首脍炙人口的五言绝句："床前明月光，疑是地上霜。举头望明月，低头思故乡。"

唐朝的雕塑艺术也很有名，主要以石雕和泥塑为主。这一时期的石雕作品，造型雄伟，做工精美，有很高的艺术价值。四川乐山的石雕大佛是唐朝的艺术精品之一，高71米，雄伟壮观，是中国最大的石雕佛像。

唐朝也是

位于四川乐山市的乐山大佛

regular rules and forms. The "modern style" poems, in terms of the number of characters in each line, were classfied into poems with five characters and with seven characters; and in terms of the number of lines, they were divided into poems

位于四川省绵阳市的李白纪念馆

consisting of four lines, eight lines and more than ten lines. *Thoughts on A Quiet Night,* a popular five-syllable poem with four lines, was written as follows: "In front of my bed is the bright moonlight, I doubt if it is the frost on the ground. I lift my head to look up at the bright moon, and lower my head to miss my hometown."

Sculpture of the Tang Dynasty was also very famous, mainly consisting of stone carvings and clay sculptures. Stone carvings of this time feature majestic poses, delicate workmanship, and high artistic value. The majestic Giant Buddha in Leshan City of Sichuan, measuring 71 meters in height, was one of the art treasures of the Tang Dynasty and the largest stone Buddha in China.

Chinese ancient painting also enjoyed rapid

长江边上的乐山大佛

中国古代绘画全面发展的时期，出现了大批优秀的画家，其中最有代表性的是吴道子和阎立本。

阎立本《步辇图》：唐太宗接见外来使者

绘画　huìhuà
to paint

吴道子　Wú Dàozǐ
an artist of the Tang Dynasty

阎立本　Yán Lìběn
an artist of the Tang Dynasty

成千上万
chéngqiān-shàngwàn
thousands of

允许　yǔnxǔ
to allow

甚至　shènzhì　even

朝廷　cháotíng
imperial court

西亚　Xīyà
West Asia

扩大　kuòdà
to enhance, to expand

沿用　yányòng
to continue to use

　　繁荣的唐朝向世界开放。当时与中国做生意的国家已经超过了70个。来自不同国家的成千上万名外国商人和留学生②长期生活在长安、洛阳等大城市。唐朝政府允许他们和中国人结婚，帮助他们开商店和饭馆，甚至还让他们在朝廷里做官。在这些外国人的帮助下，唐朝的文化和特产沿着丝绸之路传到了西亚和其他许多国家，使中国的影响力不断扩大。在海外，华人把自己生活的地方叫作"唐人街"，这个说法一直沿用到今天。

development in the Tang Dynasty, giving rise to a great number of outstanding painters. Among them the most representative ones were Wu Daozi and Yan Liben.

吴道子《八十七神仙卷》

The prosperous Tang Dynasty was open to the world. At that time, there were over 70 countries doing business with China. Thousands of foreign merchants and international students from different countries lived in Chang'an, Luoyang and other big cities. They were allowed to get married to Chinese people by the Tang government, which also provided them with assistance in opening stores and restaurants. They were even allowed to hold official positions in the imperial court. With the help of these foreigners, the

culture and specialities of the Tang Dynasty spread along the Silk Road to West Asia and many other countries, which enhanced China's influence greatly. Even today, the places where overseas Chinese people live are still referred to as "Chinatown" (literally "Tang People's Street") around the world.

美国波士顿的唐人街

文化注释

❶ 近体诗

又叫今体诗，是唐代形成的律诗和绝句的通称，和古体诗相对而言。字面意思是现代的诗，但这是对唐朝人来说的。对我们来说，"近体诗"也还是古诗。

❷ 唐朝时的来华留学生

中国的文化在唐代影响了许多国家和地区。唐代来中国留学的人达 10 万之多。"留学生"一词就起源于唐代，说的是随本国使节来中国后，留在中国学习的外国学生。

◇练习◇

▌阅读理解 Reading Comprehension

练习 1：判断正误 True（√）or false（×）

例　人们一提起唐朝，都会称赞它为"大唐盛世"。（ √ ）

1. 唐朝的中国是当时亚洲的经济和文化中心。（　　　）

2. 唐三彩是一种精美的石雕。（　　　）

3. 唐朝首都长安的人口超过了 5000 万。（　　　）

4. "西有罗马，东有长安"的意思是：罗马在西方，长安在东方。（　　　）

5. 唐朝是中国诗歌发展的黄金时代。（　　　）

6. 有文字记载的唐诗有 3 万多首。（　　　）

7. 四川乐山的石雕大佛是中国最大的石雕佛像。（　　　）

8. 唐朝时期与中国做生意的国家已经超过了 70 个。（　　　）

9. 来中国留学的人不能在中国做官。（　　　）

10. 在海外，人们把华人生活的地方叫作"唐人街"。（　　　）

练习 2：选择正确答案 Choose the right answer

例 唐朝是中国历史上最 ＿＿＿C＿＿＿ 的时期之一。

　　A. 扩大　　　　　　B. 多样　　　　　　C. 强盛　　　　　　D. 精美

1. 唐朝差不多有 ＿＿＿＿＿＿＿ 年的历史，是中国历史上最强盛的时期之一。

　　A. 300　　　　　　B. 38　　　　　　　C. 100　　　　　　D. 500

2. 人们一提起唐朝，都会称赞它为"＿＿＿＿＿＿＿"。

　　A. 繁荣强盛　　　　B. 脍炙人口　　　　C. 大唐盛世　　　　D. 东方文明

3. 唐朝的水利工程比它之前各个朝代修建的同类工程 ＿＿＿＿＿＿＿。

　　A. 总和还要多　　　B. 更加著名　　　C. 品种多样　　　D. 水平领先

4. 唐三彩是一种精美的陶器，有 ＿＿＿＿＿＿＿ 等多种颜色。

　　A. 蓝、白、绿、褐　　　　　　　　B. 黄、绿、褐、蓝

　　C. 黄、白、绿、红　　　　　　　　D. 黄、白、红、蓝

5. "西有罗马，东有长安"的说法中，"东有长安"的意思是：＿＿＿＿＿＿＿。

　　A. 长安是唐朝的首都　　　　　　B. 长安是当时东方文明的中心

　　C. 长安在世界的东方　　　　　　D. 中国的东边有长安

6. 李白、杜甫和白居易是唐朝 ＿＿＿＿＿＿＿。

　　A. 最著名的诗人　　　　　　　　B. 最优秀的画家

　　C. 水利专家　　　　　　　　　　D. 雕塑家

7. 唐诗成为最有代表性的中国古代诗歌，代表了 _____ 。

    A. 脍炙人口的五言绝句   B. 比较自由的古体诗

    C. 讲究格律的近体诗   D. 中国古代诗歌的最高成就

8. 唐朝的雕塑艺术很有名，主要以 _____ 为主。

    A. 石雕   B. 石雕和泥塑   C. 泥塑   D. 唐三彩

9. 唐朝的文化和特产沿着 _____ 传到了西亚和其他许多国家。

    A. 罗马   B. 世界各地   C. 丝绸之路   D. 唐人街

10. "唐人街" 是指 _____ 。

    A. 唐朝人修建的街区   B. 长安、洛阳等大城市

    C. 唐朝的首都   D. 海外华人生活的地方

语句练习 Sentence-Matching Exercises

连线 **Match the left side with the information on the right**

1. "大唐盛世" 是说   A. 主要以石雕和泥塑为主

2. 唐三彩   B. 沿着丝绸之路传到了许多国家

3. 唐朝的首都   C. 唐朝社会经济非常繁荣

4. 唐诗成为   D. 有黄、绿、褐、蓝等多种颜色

5. 四川乐山的石雕大佛   E. 叫作 "唐人街"

6. 唐朝的雕塑艺术   F. 长期生活在长安

7. 吴道子和阎立本是   G. 是唐朝的雕塑艺术精品之一

8. 唐朝的文化和特产   H. 最有代表性的中国古代诗歌

9. 海外华人生活的地方   I. 是当时的国际性大都市

10. 成千上万名外国商人和留学生   J. 唐朝优秀的画家

三 词汇练习 Vocabulary Exercises

用课文中学过的词语填空 Fill in the blanks with words/expressions in this lesson

强盛	繁荣	超过	手工业	陶器
空前	记载	雕塑	绘画	扩大

　　唐朝是中国历史上最　<u>强盛</u>　的时期之一。 那时候，中国社会安定，经济发达，国力强大，历史上把这个时期叫作"大唐盛世"。唐朝的＿＿＿＿表现在哪些方面呢？首先，唐朝的经济繁荣程度＿＿＿＿了以往任何一个朝代。当时的＿＿＿＿和工艺也很发达，不但品种多样，而且达到了世界领先水平。唐三彩就是一个最好的例子。唐三彩是一种精美的＿＿＿＿，有黄、绿、褐、蓝等多种颜色，形象生动，色彩鲜艳，在唐朝的时候就已经销售到世界各地。唐朝的＿＿＿＿艺术也很有名，主要以石雕和泥塑为主。四川乐山的石雕大佛是唐朝的艺术精品之一，是中国最大的石雕佛像。除了手工业和工艺以外，唐朝在文学和艺术方面的成就也是＿＿＿＿的。唐诗是最有代表性的中国古代诗歌，有文字＿＿＿＿的唐诗近5万首。唐朝也是中国古代＿＿＿＿全面发展的时期，出现了大批优秀的画家。随着经济的繁荣，中国的影响力不断＿＿＿＿，唐朝的文化和特产传到了世界上许多国家。

四 语法练习 Grammar Exercises

用所给的词语组句 Make sentences with the words and phrases given

例　之一　唐朝　最强盛的　是　时期　中国历史上
　　唐朝是中国历史上最强盛的时期之一。

1. 在世界上　有着　十分　地位　中国　重要的　唐朝时期的

   _____

2. 工艺　唐朝的　达到了　品种多样　领先水平　不但　手工业　和　而且
   世界

   _____

3. 是　中国　黄金时代　唐朝　诗歌　发展的

   _____

4. 以……为主　石雕和泥塑　唐朝的　很有名　雕塑艺术　主要　也

   _____

5. 文化　沿着　传到了　丝绸之路　特产　其他许多国家　唐朝的　和

   _____

五 写作练习 Writing Practice

用下列词语造句 **Make sentences using the following words/phrases/structures**

1. 光是……就……：_____

2. 比……还要多：_____

3. 达到了……水平：_____

4. 出自……之手：_____

5. 脍炙人口：_____

6. 以……为主：_____

7. 壮观：_____

8. 成千上万：_____

9. 允许：_____

10. 在……的帮助下：_____

玄奘取经 6

Xuánzàng, **Xuanzang** (602–664), a Buddhist monk of the Tang Dynasty

qǔ jīng, to go on a pilgrimage for Buddhist scriptures

中国著名电视剧《西游记》

导读问题　Lead-in Questions

1. 上图中的人物你知道吗？
2. 你看过《西游记（Xīyóu Jì, *Journey to the West*）》吗？你知道故事的原型（yuánxíng, prototype）是什么样的吗？
3. 玄奘为什么去天竺（Tiānzhú, ancient India）？他在天竺住了多少年？
4. 玄奘对中国佛教（Fójiào, Buddhism）的贡献（gòngxiàn, contribution）是什么？
5. 《西游记》为什么在中国家喻户晓（jiāyù-hùxiǎo, known to every household）？

高僧	gāosēng	
eminent or senior monk		
佛经	fójīng	
the Buddhist scriptures		
僧人	sēngrén	
monk		
佛法	fófǎ	
Buddhism		
印度	Yìndù	
India		
皇帝	huángdì	
emperor		
私自	sīzì	
privately		
长安	Cháng'ān	
the capital of the Tang Dynasty, the present-day Xi'an		
南亚	Nányà	
South Asia		
中亚	Zhōngyà	
Central Asia		
阿富汗	Āfùhàn	
Afghanistan		
巴基斯坦	Bājīsītǎn	
Pakistan		
安宁	ānníng	
peaceful		
使命	shǐmìng	
mission		

玄奘是中国唐朝著名的高僧，也是中国伟大的佛经翻译家和旅行家。为了帮助僧人们更好地理解佛法，他决定去天竺，也就是今天的印度，学习那里的佛法。天竺在中国的西边，离中国非常远。玄奘要去那儿，必须经过皇帝同意才行。可是当他请求皇帝让他去天竺时，皇帝却不同意。但是，玄奘已经下定了决心，要学到真正的佛法，所以他就私自离开长安往西边的天竺去了。

向西走的路上，玄奘穿过了大片沙漠，经过了许多地方，包括今天的南亚、中亚部分国家和地区，比如阿富汗、巴基斯坦、印度等国，玄奘受到了他们的欢迎和喜爱。有一个国家的国王还想把玄奘留下来，为他的国家和人民求得安宁。但玄奘没有忘记自己的理想和使命，那就是要去更远的天竺学习真正的佛法，所以他不愿意留在这个国家，不愿意放弃自己取经的计划，于是就继续往天竺的方向走。

玄奘画像

Xuanzang was an eminent monk of China's Tang Dynasty, as well as a great Buddhist sutra translator and traveler. In order to help monks better comprehend Buddhist doctrine, he decided to go to Tianzhu, the present-day India, to study the Buddhism there. Tianzhu was located on the west of the Tang empire and was very far away from it. Xuanzang needed to

中国西部的沙漠

receive the emperor's consent to go there, but his request was disapproved by the emperor. However, Xuanzang had already made up his mind to study genuine Buddhism, so he left Chang'an and went westwards to Tianzhu without permission.

On his way to the west, Xuanzang went through deserts and passed many places, including some countries and regions in today's South Asia and Central Asia, such as Afghanistan, Pakistan, India, and other countries. Xuanzang received their welcome and adoration. A king of a country hoped that Xuanzang would stay there and acquire peace for his country and

people. But Xuanzang did not forget his mission, which was to go even further to Tianzhu to study genuine Buddhism. He did not want to stay in that country, nor did he want to give up his plan to study Buddhism in Tianzhu, so he continued his journey

玄奘西行路上的古城遗址

寺庙　sìmiào
temple

钦佩　qīnpèi
to respect, to admire

欣赏　xīnshǎng
to appreciate, to enjoy

挑选　tiāoxuǎn
to select

西安大雁塔前的玄奘雕像

唐太宗　Táng Tàizōng
the second emperor of the
Tang Dynasty, i.e., Li Shimin

称赞　chēngzàn
to praise, to commend

在克服了各种困难之后，玄奘终于到达了天竺国。

在那儿他认识了许多高僧，并常常跟着这些高僧学习佛法，一有问题就向他们请教。在天竺的寺庙里他学到了许多东西，看到了以前没有看过的佛经，经常和其他的僧人讨论佛法。因为玄奘在天竺学习佛法很认真，取得了很好的成绩，所以他在天竺成了一位非常著名的佛法大师。许多僧人都知道他、钦佩他，因为他们都觉得玄奘对佛法的理解比他们还好，连天竺的国王都非常欣赏他，想把他留在这里。可是，离开中国已经十几年了，玄奘想回到中国，把他在天竺学到的佛法带回去，让中国人也知道什么是真正的佛法。所以他在天竺用心挑选了许多佛经，把它们带回了中国。

回到中国以后，玄奘受到唐太宗和长安市民的热烈欢迎，唐太宗不但称赞

玄奘收藏佛经、佛像的大雁塔，位于西安

to Tianzhu. After having overcomed all sorts of difficulties and hardships, Xuanzang finally arrived in Tianzhu.

There he met many eminent monks and studied Buddhist doctrine along with them, asking these eminent monks for advice whenever he had a question. In the monasteries of Tianzhu, he learned a lot, read scriptures he had never read, and often discussed Buddhism with other monks. Because Xuanzang studied Buddhism earnestly in Tianzhu, many monks heard about him and

玄奘曾经学习过的那烂陀遗址

admired him since they all believed Xuanzang's understanding of Buddhism was even better than theirs. Even the King of Tianzhu admired him very much and hoped he could stay in his country. But Xuanzang had been gone from the Tang empire for over ten years; he wanted to return to the Tang empire, bring back the Buddhism he studied in Tianzhu, and help his people learn what real Buddhism was. So in Tianzhu, he carefully selected many scriptures and brought them back to the Tang empire.

After returning to the Tang empire, Xuanzang received a warm welcome from the Emperor Tangtaizong and the people of Chang'an City. Not only did the emperor

唐太宗称赞玄奘而写的《大唐三藏圣教序》

当时	dāngshí	at that time
建造	jiànzào	
to build, to construct		
越南	Yuènán	Vietnam
感人	gǎnrén	moving
谈论	tánlùn	to talk about
甚至	shènzhì	even
吴承恩	Wú Chéng'ēn	

a novelist and poet of the Ming Dynasty (1368–1644), generally acknowledged as the author of the classic Chinese novel *Journey to the West*

孙悟空　Sūn Wùkōng
Monkey King

猪八戒　Zhū Bājiè
Monk Pig—one of the three disciples of Xuanzang in the classic Chinese novel *Journey to the West*

沙和尚　Shā héshang
Sand Monk—one of the three disciples of Xuanzang in the classic Chinese novel *Journey to the West*

唐僧　Tángsēng
one of the heroes in the classic Chinese novel *Journey to the West*. The character is based on the historical Buddhist monk Xuanzang

西天　Xītiān
ancient India, Western Paradise

拍电影　pāi diànyǐng
to shoot a film

了玄奘，还同意玄奘在当时的首都长安建造一个翻译佛经的地方①。后来，这些佛经还被传到了日本、朝鲜和越南。

　　玄奘取经的感人故事成了人们喜欢谈论的话题。人们把他去天竺取经的经历编成故事，这些故事越讲越多，越传越广，慢慢地，民间甚至把玄奘去天竺取经的经历编成了神话故事。明朝的时候，有一个叫吴承恩的作家把这些神话故事编成一本书，书名叫《西游记》，书中描写了孙悟空、猪八戒、沙和尚是如何克服各种困难，保护唐僧玄奘到西天取经的。如今，《西游记》的故事被拍成了电影、电视剧，可以说在中国家喻户晓。

电视剧《西游记》

Tangtaizong commend Xuanzang, but also consented Xuanzang to build a pagoda to translate the Buddhist scriptures in Chang'an, the capital of the Tang Dynasty at that time. Afterwards, these scriptures were spread to Japan, Korea, and Vietnam.

The moving stories about Xuanzang's journey to the West to study Buddhism became a topic people loved to talk about. Some people composed stories based on his experiences. With these stories growing in number and popularity, they were gradually turned into fairy tales. In the Ming Dynasty,

《西游记》作者吴承恩雕像

there was an author named Wu Cheng'en who wrote a book based on these stories, which was known as *Journey to the West*. It told the stories about all the difficulties that the Monkey King, Monk Pig, and Sand Monk overcame to protect Xuanzang on his journey to the West. Nowadays, *Journey to the West* has been made into movies and television series and is known to every household in China.

孙悟空的扮演者六小龄童

77

文化注释

❶ 翻译佛经的地方

　　即大雁塔，位于今天的西安市，建于公元 652 年，是玄奘为收藏佛经、佛像而主持修建的。今天看到的塔共七层，高 64 米，是古都西安的标志性建筑。

◇ 练习 ◇

■ 阅读理解 Reading Comprehension

练习 1：判断正误 True(√) or false(×)

例　玄奘是中国明朝著名的法师，也是伟大的佛经翻译家。(×)

1. 为了学到真正的佛法，玄奘决定去西边的天竺。(　　)

2. 皇帝同意以后，玄奘才离开长安前往天竺。(　　)

3. 在向西走的路上，玄奘经过了许多地方。(　　)

4. 有一个国家的国王要玄奘去天竺，为他的国家和人民求得安宁。(　　)

5. 玄奘一有问题就向天竺的国王请教。(　　)

6. 玄奘在天竺学习佛法很认真，取得了很好的成绩。(　　)

7. 天竺的许多僧人都很钦佩玄奘。(　　)

8. 玄奘把用心挑选的佛经带回了中国。(　　)

9. 后来，这些佛经还被传到了日本、朝鲜和越南。(　　)

10.《西游记》说的是天竺国佛教的故事。(　　)

练习 2：选择正确答案 **Choose the right answer**

例 玄奘是中国唐朝著名的 ＿＿＿B＿＿＿，也是伟大的旅行家。

  A. 诗人 　　　　B. 佛经翻译家 　　C. 画家 　　　　D. 雕塑家

1. 为了＿＿＿＿＿，玄奘决定去天竺，学习那里的佛教。

  A. 帮助僧人们更好地理解佛法 　　B. 传播中国的佛教

  C. 远途旅行 　　　　　　　　　　D. 访问天竺国

2. 皇帝不让玄奘去天竺，但是玄奘决定＿＿＿＿＿＿。

  A. 私自离开长安去西边的天竺 　　B. 等待皇帝的答复

  C. 跟皇帝一起去天竺 　　　　　　D. 以后再去天竺

3. 在向天竺走的路上，玄奘经过了许多国家，＿＿＿＿＿＿。

  A. 见到了很多国王 　　　　　　　B. 和僧人们讨论佛法

  C. 买了很多佛经 　　　　　　　　D. 受到了他们的欢迎和喜爱

4. 有一个国家的国王想留下玄奘，但他没同意，因为＿＿＿＿＿＿。

  A. 他不喜欢这些国家 　　　　　　B. 他不愿意放弃自己取经的计划

  C. 当地的人们不信仰佛教 　　　　D. 这些国家比中国小得多

5. ＿＿＿＿＿＿，所以取得了很好的成绩。

  A. 天竺国王很欣赏他 　　　　　　B. 玄奘克服了很多困难

  C. 玄奘很有名 　　　　　　　　　D. 玄奘学习佛法很认真

6. 许多天竺的僧人都觉得玄奘＿＿＿＿＿＿。

  A. 喜欢帮助别人 　　　　　　　　B. 对佛教的理解比他们还好

  C. 没看过佛经 　　　　　　　　　D. 不懂佛法

7. 十几年过去了，玄奘想回到中国，_____ 。

    A. 把在天竺用心挑选的佛经带回中国   B. 把天竺的僧人带回中国

    C. 看望自己的家人和朋友   D. 跟其他僧人一起学习佛经

8. 回到中国以后，玄奘受到了 _____ 和长安市民的称赞。

    A. 天竺高僧   B. 天竺国王   C. 唐太宗   D. 李白

9. _____ 传到了日本、朝鲜和越南。

    A. 玄奘翻译的佛经   B. 翻译佛经的故事

    C. 玄奘挑选的佛经   D. 吴承恩写《西游记》这件事

10. 慢慢地，民间把玄奘去天竺取经的经历编成了_____ 。

    A. 佛经   B. 歌曲   C. 神话故事   D. 一本书

▤ 语句练习 Sentence-Matching Exercises

连线 **Match the left side with the information on the right**

1. 为了帮助僧人们更好地理解佛法   A. 所以就继续向西走

2. 玄奘经过了很多国家   B. 带回了中国

3. 他不愿意留在那个国家   C. 成了人们喜欢谈论的话题

4. 天竺在中国的西边   D. 受到了他们的欢迎和喜爱

5. 克服了各种困难之后   E. 离中国非常远

6. 他在天竺用心挑选了许多佛经   F. 玄奘决定去天竺，学习那里的佛教

7. 这些佛经还被传到了   G. 被拍成了电影、电视，在中国家喻户晓

8. 玄奘取经的感人故事   H. 把玄奘取经的故事编成了一本书

9. 有一个叫吴承恩的作家   I. 日本、朝鲜和越南

10. 《西游记》的故事   J. 玄奘终于到达了天竺国

三 词汇练习 Vocabulary Exercises

用课文中学过的词语填空 **Fill in the blanks with words/expressions in this lesson**

伟大	佛经	高僧	寺庙	成绩
佛法	钦佩	挑选	谈论	西游记

　　玄奘是中国唐朝著名的　高僧　，也是　　　　　　的佛经翻译家和旅行家。为了帮助僧人们更好地理解　　　　　　，他决定去天竺学习。天竺在中国的西边，离中国非常远，虽然皇帝不同意，但玄奘下定决心一个人去天竺。路上，他经过了许多国家，受到了他们的欢迎和喜爱。在克服了各种困难之后，玄奘终于到达了天竺国。他每天都跟着天竺的高僧学习佛法。在天竺的　　　　　里，他看到了以前没有看过的　　　　　　。玄奘认真地学习佛法，取得了很好的　　　　　　，对佛经的理解越来越好，许多僧人都知道他、　　　　　　他。离开中国已经十几年了，玄奘决定回中国去。他用心　　　　　　了许多佛经带回中国。后来，这些佛经还被传到了日本、朝鲜和越南。玄奘取经的感人故事成了人们喜欢　　　　　　的话题。这些故事越讲越多，越传越广。后来，有一个叫吴承恩的作家把这些故事编成了一本书，书名叫《　　　　　　》。

四 语法练习 Grammar Exercises

用所给的词语组句 **Make sentences with the words and phrases given**

例　高僧　佛经翻译家和旅行家　玄奘　是　也是　中国唐朝　著名的
中国伟大的

玄奘是中国唐朝著名的高僧，也是中国伟大的佛经翻译家和旅行家。

1. 天竺　玄奘　去了　决心　西边的　私自出国　下定了　往

2. 天竺的　他　国王　都　欣赏　很　连

_____

3. 玄奘　回到　中国　想　让　佛法　中国人　知道　真正的　什么是

_____

4. 人们　玄奘　去天竺　经历　编成　故事　把　取经的

_____

5. 家喻户晓　拍成了　被　电影、电视剧　可以说　在中国　《西游记》的故事

_____

五 写作练习 Writing Practice

用下列词语造句 Make sentences using the following words/phrases/structures

1. 必须……才……：_____

2. 私自：_____

3. 于是：_____

4. 一……就……：_____

5. 钦佩：_____

6. 连……都……：_____

7. 越……越……：_____

8. 慢慢地：_____

9. 如何：_____

10. 家喻户晓：_____

四大发明

指南针

火药

造纸术

活字印刷术

导读问题　Lead-in Questions

1. 你听说过中国的四大发明吗？它们是什么？

2. 中国人是什么时候发现有磁性（cíxìng, magnetism）的东西可以用来指方向的？

3. 火药（huǒyào, gunpowder）是怎样发明的？造纸术（zàozhǐshù, paper-making technology）是谁发明的？

4. 活字印刷术（huózì yìnshuāshù, movable-type printing）为什么是印刷（yìnshuā, to print）史上的重要发明？

5. 为什么说中国的四大发明对世界文明做出了巨大（jùdà, huge, mighty）贡献（gòngxiàn, contribution）？

提起 tíqǐ
to mention

神奇 shénqí
magic

悠久 yōujiǔ
long

壮美 zhuàngměi
magnificent and beautiful

云海 yúnhǎi
sea of clouds

翻飞 fānfēi
to swirl

神龙 shénlóng
divine dragon

关键词 guānjiàncí
keyword

耀眼 yàoyǎn
dazzling

指南针 zhǐnánzhēn
compass

光滑 guānghuá
smooth

铜盘 tóngpán
copper plate

转动 zhuàndòng
to rotate

指向 zhǐxiàng
to point

固定 gùdìng
to fix

航海 hánghǎi
to navigate on the sea

提起中国，你最先想到的是什么？神奇的功夫、悠久的历史、壮美的山水，还是在云海间翻飞的神龙？在关于中国的众多关键词中，有一个词格外耀眼，那就是"发明"。你知道中国人发明的哪些东西影响了整个世界吗？你知道中国历史上都有哪些伟大的发明家吗？今天让我们一起来了解中国古代的四大发明吧，那就是指南针、火药、造纸术和活字印刷术。

先说说指南针吧。两千多年以前，中国人就发现有磁性的东西可以用来指示

最古老的指南针：司南

方向。他们把一个形状像勺子、底部光滑的磁石放在又平又滑的铜盘上，让它自由转动，磁石停下来的时候，它尖尖的一端总是指向南方。这就是最早的指南针。后来，人们造出了铁针。他们把铁针做成磁针，用一根很细的线把磁针固定在一个光滑的盘上面。盘上刻有不同的方向，磁针总是指着南方。这样，一个真正的指南针就形成了。北宋时期，指南针开始用于航海。安装在海船

When China is mentioned, what is the very first thing you think of? Is it the magic kung fu, the long history, the magnificent scenery, or a divine dragon swirling in the sea of clouds? Among the many keywords related to China, one is particularly noteworthy, that

中国功夫

is, "inventions". Do you know what Chinese inventions have influenced the whole world? Do you know what great inventors there were in Chinese history? Today, let's talk about the Four Great Inventions of ancient China, which are compass, gunpowder, paper-making, and movable-type printing.

Let's talk about the compass first. Over 2,000 years ago, Chinese people discovered that magnetic things could be used to point to a direction. They put a ladle shaped magnet with a smooth bottom on a flat and smooth copper plate, letting it rotate freely. When the magnet stopped, its tip always pointed south. This was the earliest compass. Later, people made an iron needle; they made the needle magnetic and used a thin thread to fasten the needle

onto the top of a smooth plate, on which directions were carved. For the magnetic needle always pointed south, a compass in the real sense took shape. In the North Song Dynasty, the compass began to be used for navigation. Compasses installed on ships were referred to as Luopan. A

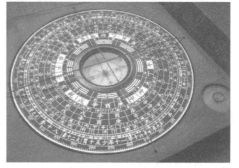

罗盘

罗盘	luópán	compass
迷失	míshī	
to lose (one's direction)		
航行	hángxíng	to sail
炼	liàn	to refine
长生不老		
chángshēng bù lǎo		
to become immortal		
仙丹	xiāndān	elixir of life
爆炸	bàozhà	to explode
硫磺	liúhuáng	sulfur
硝石	xiāoshí	saltpeter
木炭	mùtàn	charcoal
混合	hùnhé	
to blend, to mix		
加热	jiārè	to heat
开采	kāicǎi	to mine
烟花	yānhuā	firework
爆竹	bàozhú	firecracker
战争	zhànzhēng	war, battle
枪炮	qiāngpào	firearm
攻击	gōngjī	to attack
公元	gōngyuán	
Christian era		
蔡伦	Cài Lún	
inventor of paper		
树皮	shùpí	tree bark
破布	pò bù	rag
煮	zhǔ	to boil
浆	jiāng	pulp

上的指南针叫罗盘。不管白天还是黑夜，只要有了罗盘，船就不会迷失方向，海上航行就安全多了。

再说说火药。中国古时候有些人梦想炼出可以让人长生不老的"仙丹"①。有时候，炼"仙丹"的炉子会发生爆炸。后来人们发现，硫磺、硝石和木炭按一定的比例混合在一起并且加热就会发生爆炸。这三种东西的混合物就是火药。火药可以用来开采石头，也可以做成节日用的烟花和爆竹。战争的时候，人们用火药制成枪炮，攻击敌人。

另外一项中国古代的发明是造纸术。东汉时期（公元25年～公元220年）有个叫蔡伦的人，想造出一种又好又便宜、可以写字的东西。他试验了各种各样的原料，最后发现，把树皮和破布一起煮成浆，经过多

中国人喜欢用烟花庆祝节日

ship would not lose its directions at any time as long as a compass was used. Thus sea navigation became much safer.

Next, let's talk about gunpowder. In ancient China, some people wished to refine the "elixir of life" from some substances to help people become immortal. Sometimes, the stove refining the pills exploded. Afterwards, people found out that if sulfur, saltpeter and charcoal in certain proportions were mixed together and heated, the stove would explode. The mixture of these three things was known as gunpowder, which could be used to break rocks, and make the fireworks and firecrackers needed on festivals. When a war broke out, gunpowder was used to manufacture firearms to attack enemies.

Another ancient Chinese invention was paper-making technology. In the Eastern Han Dynasty (25 AD–220 AD), a man named Cai Lun wanted to make something on which characters could be written nicely and conveniently. He experimented with

炼丹的炉子

蔡伦雕像

工艺　gōngyì
technology, craftmanship

毕昇雕像

字盘　zìpán
character board
排列　páiliè
to arrange
从此　cóngcǐ
since then
印度　Yìndù
India

种工艺，就可以制成又轻又光滑的纸。这种纸很便宜，便于普及。

四大发明的最后一项就是活字印刷术。在活字印刷术发明之前，人们必须把需要印刷的字一个一个地刻在一块木板上②。可是因为每个字都是不能活动的，所以，印刷不同的内容就需要刻不同的木板，非常麻烦。北宋时期（公元 960 年～公元 1127 年），有个叫毕昇的人，试了很多次，做成了可以活动的字。印刷的时候，把字一个一个地排在字盘上；印好以后，把它们取下来重新排列，就可以再次印刷。从此以后，印书就变得又快又简单了。

字盘

中国古代的四大发明不久就都传到了日本、印度等国家，后来又传到欧洲，影响了整个世界。因此，四大发明不但对中国文明做出了巨大的贡献，也对世界古代文明做出了巨大贡献。可以说，我们能有当今世界诸多发达的科技成果，也有四大发明的一份功劳。

all sorts of raw materials, and finally found out that light and smooth paper could be made if tree barks and rags were boiled together into pulp and went

through many other procedures. Being inexpensive, this kind of paper was easy to be popularized.

雕版印刷需要把字一个一个地刻在木板上

The last of the Four Great Inventions is movable-type printing. Before it was invented, people had to carve the charac-ters needed one by one on a wooden block. However, since each cha-racter could not be moved, printing different contents required people to carve different wooden blocks, which was extremely troublesome. In the Northern Song Dynasty (960 AD-1127 AD), a man named Bi Sheng made movable-type characters after many experiments. Before printing, characters were arranged on a board; after printing, they were rearranged and reprinted. After that, printing became much quicker and simpler.

活字印刷

The Four Great Inventions of ancient China were quickly spread to other countries like Japan and India; later they were spread to Europe and influenced the whole world. As a result, the Four Great Chinese Inventions made a great contribution not only to the Chinese civilization, but also to the ancient civilization of the world. It is true to say that China's Four Great Inventions should be credited for their contribution to the great achievements in science and technology in the world today.

文化注释

❶ 仙丹

　　传说是一种长生不老药。在中国历史上的秦、汉、南北朝时期，皇帝为了保住江山、富贵、权力，很多都曾经到处寻找长生不老、延年益寿的灵丹妙药 —— 仙丹。

❷ 雕版印刷

　　这是最早在中国出现的印刷形式。现存最早的雕版印刷品是敦煌莫高窟发现的印制于公元 868 年的《金刚经》（现存于大英博物馆）。

◇ 练习 ◇

▌阅读理解 Reading Comprehension

练习 1：判断正误 True（√）or false（×）

例　中国的四大发明闻名世界。（ √ ）

1. 中国古代的四大发明是：指南针、火药、造纸术和活字印刷术。（　　　）

2. 指南针是上个世纪发明的。（　　　）

3. 安装在汽车上的指南针叫罗盘。（　　　）

4. 火药的出现与古人炼"仙丹"有关。（　　　）

5. 火药可以做成节日用的烟花和爆竹。（　　　）

6. 造纸术是唐朝发明的。（　　　）

7. 发明活字印刷术的人是东汉时期的毕昇。（　　　）

8. 使用活字印刷以后，印书就变得又快又简单了。（　　　）

9. 中国古代的四大发明不久就都传到了日本、印度等国家。（　　　）

10. 中国古代的四大发明都出现在北宋时期。（　　　）

例　___C___，指南针开始用于航海。

　A. 两千多年以前　　B. 东汉时期　　C. 北宋时期　　　　D. 唐朝

1. 两千多年以前，中国人就发现有磁性的东西可以_____。

　A. 发光　　　　　B. 有引力　　　C. 用来指示方向　　D. 爆炸

2. 安装在海船上的指南针叫_____。

　A. 罗盘　　　　　B. 铁针　　　　C. 方向盘　　　　　D. 磁石

3. _____有了罗盘，船_____不会迷失方向，海上航行就安全多了。

　A. 只有……才……　　　　　　B. 只要……就……

　C. 不仅……而且……　　　　　D. 虽然……但是……

4. "仙丹"是中国古时候人们梦想的_____。

　A. 神仙喝的水　　B. 野生草药　　C. 长生不老药　　D. 皇帝用的药材

5. _____按一定比例的混合物就是火药。

　A. 硫磺、硝石和木炭　　　　　B. 硫磺、爆竹和木炭

　C. 硝石、烟花和木炭　　　　　D. 硝石、爆竹和纸浆

6. 火药可以用来_____。

　A. 开采石头　　　　　　　　　B. 做成节日用的烟花和爆竹

　C. 制成枪炮　　　　　　　　　D. A、B 和 C

7. 蔡伦发现，把树皮和破布一起_____，经过多种工艺，就可以制成又轻又光滑的纸。

A. 放在草地上　　B. 放在桌子上　　C. 混合并加热　　D. 煮成浆

8. 在发明活字印刷之前，人们必须把需要印刷的字_____。

　　A. 重新排列　　　　　　　　B. 排在字盘上

　　C. 写在纸上　　　　　　　　D. 刻在木板上

9. 活字印刷就是把可以活动的字_____。

　　A. 重新排列，再次印刷　　　B. 印在纸上

　　C. 放在不同的木板上　　　　D. 雕刻在木板上

10. 中国古代的四大发明不久就都传到了_____。

　　A. 日本　　　　B. 美国　　　　C. 地中海　　　　D. 非洲

语句练习 Sentence-Matching Exercises

连线 **Match the left side with the information on the right**

1. 中国古代的四大发明　　　　　A. 开采石头，做烟花、爆竹

2. 中国人发现有磁性的　　　　　B. 树皮和破布一起煮成的浆
　　东西可以用来指示方向

3. 指南针安装在海船上　　　　　C. 于是就发明了指南针

4. 火药可以用来　　　　　　　　D. 人们把需要印刷的字刻在木板上

5. 战争的时候　　　　　　　　　E. 发明了活字印刷术

6. 东汉时期有个叫蔡伦的人　　　F. 人们用火药制成枪炮，攻击敌人

7. 古代造纸的原料是　　　　　　G. 闻名世界

8. 在发明活字印刷术之前　　　　H. 可以重新排列，再次印刷

9. 北宋时期，有个叫毕昇的人　　　I. 发明了造纸术

10. 活动的字，在印刷时　　　　　J. 船就不会迷失方向

三 词汇练习 Vocabulary Exercises

用课文中学过的词语填空 **Fill in the blanks with words/expressions in this lesson**

指南针	磁性	印刷术	航海	爆炸
工艺	混合	仙丹	排列	贡献

　　中国古代的四大发明是：__指南针__、火药、造纸术和活字_____。两千多年前，中国人就发现有_____的东西可以用来指示方向。北宋时期，指南针开始用于_____。古人在炼可以让人长生不老的"_____"时发现，硫磺、硝石和木炭按一定的比例_____在一起并且加热就会发生_____，于是就发明了火药。发明造纸术的人叫蔡伦。他把树皮和破布一起煮成浆，经过多种_____，就可以制成又轻又光滑的纸。最后一项发明是活字印刷。北宋时期的毕昇做了可以活动的字，这些字可以重新_____，也可以再次印刷。从此以后，印书就变得又快又简单了。不久，中国古代的四大发明就都传到了日本、印度等国家，后来影响了整个世界，对世界古代文明做出了巨大_____。

四 语法练习 Grammar Exercises

用所给的词语组句 **Make sentences with the words and phrases given**

例　罗盘　只要……就……　方向　不会　迷失　有了　船
　　只要有了罗盘，船就不会迷失方向。

1.哪些　你　有　知道　发明家　中国历史上　吗　伟大的

_____

2. 它尖尖的　停下来　指向　一端　总是　南方　磁石　的时候

_____

3. 梦想　有些人　长生不老　可以让人　"仙丹"　炼出　的

_____

4. 火药　开采　也可以　节日用的　做成　烟花和爆竹　可以　用来　石头

_____

5. 又轻又光滑的　把树皮和破布　纸　一起　可以制成　煮成浆　就

_____

五 写作练习 Writing Practice

用下列词语造句 **Make sentences using the following words/phrases/structures**

1. 提起……：_____

2. 悠久：_____

3. 格外：_____

4. 不管……还是……：_____

5. 只要……就……：_____

6. 可以……也可以……：_____

7. 又……又……：_____

8. 便于：_____

9. 因为……所以……：_____

10. 从此：_____

丝绸之路 8

> Sīchóu Zhī Lù, Silk Road, an ancient network of trade routes connecting the West and the East from China to the Mediterranean Sea

汉朝张骞出使西域

导读问题 Lead-in Questions

1. 你知道著名的丝绸之路吗？上图中的人物和丝绸之路有什么关系？
2. 丝绸之路经过了哪些国家？
3. 商人们沿着（yánzhe, along...）丝绸之路，把什么货物（huòwù, product, goods）运到西方？又把什么货物带回中国？
4. 除了食物，还有什么重要的东西通过丝绸之路传进了中国？
5. 为什么说丝绸之路是亚洲（Yàzhōu, Asia）和欧洲各国经济文化交流的友谊（yǒuyì, friendship）之路？

古老	gǔlǎo	old, ancient
商路	shānglù	trade route
长安	Cháng'ān	the capital

of the Tang Dynasty, the present-day Xi'an

起点	qǐdiǎn	starting point
甘肃	Gānsù	

one of the provinces in China

新疆	Xīnjiāng	

one of the five autonomous regions in China

中亚	Zhōngyà	

Central Asia

西亚	Xīyà	West Asia
连接	liánjiē	to connect
地中海	Dìzhōng Hǎi	

the Mediterranean Sea

丝绸	sīchóu	silk
开辟	kāipì	to open up
张骞	Zhāng Qiān	

a diplomatic envoy of the Han Dynasty

公元	gōngyuán	

Christian era

官员	guānyuán	official
当时	dāngshí	at that time
相互	xiānghù	mutual
增进	zēngjìn	to enhance
皇帝	huángdì	emperor
派	pài	

to send (someone on mission)

丝绸之路是中国西北部一条非常古老的商路。它全长大约七千公里，以长安（现在的陕西省西安市）为起点，经过甘肃、新疆，到达中亚、西亚，进而连接地中海各国。大约在一千多年前，人们就开始通过这条路，将中国出产的货物运到欧洲。因为货物中丝绸产品最多、影响最大，因此这条商路就被称为"丝绸之路"。

走在丝绸之路上的骆驼队

那么，第一个开辟丝绸之路的人是谁呢？这个人叫张骞。张骞本人并不是商人，而是中国汉朝（公元前206年～公元220年）的一位官员。当时中国和西边的国家相互之间都不了解，为了增进国家之间的交往，皇帝就派他去访问这些国家。公元前2世纪，张骞带领一百多人出发了。一路上，他们遇到了很多困难，十多年后终于到达了那些

The Silk Road was a very old trade route in northwestern China. Its total length measured approximately 7,000 kilometers, starting from Chang'an (today's Xi'an in Shaanxi Province), going through Gansu and Xinjiang to Central Asia and West Asia, thus connecting the countries

丝绸之路遗址

around the Mediterranean Sea. Over a thousand years ago, products were transported from China to Europe on this road. Since silk products were the most numerous and influential among others, this trade route became known as the Silk Road.

Then, who opened up the Silk Road? It was Zhang Qian, who was actually not a merchant, but an official of China's Han Dynasty (206 BC–220 AD). At that time, there was no mutual understanding between China and the countries on the west of it. To promote the contacts with

张骞雕像

97

地理　dìlǐ　geography

物产　wùchǎn　product

风俗习惯　fēngsú xíguàn
folk customs

详细　xiángxì　detailed

出使　chūshǐ
to serve as an envoy abroad

西域　Xīyù
West Region , today's Xinjiang
Uygur Autonomous Region
and the areas west to it

率领　shuàilǐng　to lead

使者　shǐzhě
envoy, messenger

回访　huífǎng
to pay a visit back

从此　cóngcǐ　since then

频繁　pínfán　frequently

政治　zhèngzhì　politics

骆驼　luòtuo　camel

丝绸做的旗袍

国家，对当地的地理、物产、风俗习惯有了比较详细的了解。这些国家的人也通过张骞了解了中国。这就是中国历史上有名的"张骞出使西域"。公元前119年，张骞第二次出使西域。他率领使团，带着上万头牛羊和大量丝绸，访

丝绸之路上运送货物的驼队

问西域的许多国家。西域各国也派使者回访长安。中国和西域的交往从此越来越频繁，从而加强了西域各国与中国在政治、经济、文化上的联系。

张骞使中国和西域各国之间第一次建立了联系。张骞开辟了这条丝绸之路以后，很多商人就沿着张骞走过的路线，把中国的货物用马和骆驼运到西边的国家。他们从当时中国的首都长安出发，向西经过很多的国家，最远到达过地中海地区。他们走到哪里，就把中国的货物卖到哪里。那个时候，欧洲人和中亚人非常喜欢中国的丝绸，但他们自己却不会生产，所以丝绸在这些国家很受欢迎，但价格非常贵，只有

these countries, the emperor sent him to visit these countries. In the 2nd century BC, Zhang Qian set off leading over a hundred people. Having encountered many difficulties on their journey, they finally arrived in these countries after over ten years, and got relatively detailed information

丝绸之路上的主要商品——丝绸

on the geography, products, and folk customs of these countries. The People in these countries also learned about China from Zhang Qian. This was the famous story of "Zhang Qian going west as a diplomatic envoy" in Chinese history. In 119 BC, Zhang Qian went west for the second time. He led a diplomatic team, taking thousands of cows and sheep and a great amount of silk with him to visit many countries in the West Region (today's Xinjiang Uygur Autonomous Region and the areas on the west of it). The countries of the West Region also sent envoys to visit Chang'an. Since then, China had more frequent contact with the West Region, thus strengthening the political, economic and cultural links between them.

Zhang Qian established the first contact between China and the countries in the West Region. After he opened up the Silk Road, many merchants, following the route Zhang Qian traveled, transported Chinese

丝绸之路上的主要商品——茶叶

瓷器　cíqì
porcelain

造纸　zào zhǐ
to make paper

印刷　yìnshuā
to print

最终　zuìzhōng
finally

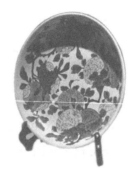

陶瓷盘子

很有钱的人才买得起。除了丝绸，商人们还把中国的瓷器、茶叶等运到西方，卖给当地人。

当时，西方人并不知道如何造纸，也不懂得怎样印刷。而造纸术和印刷术都是中国发明的，所以造纸和印刷的方法也沿着丝绸之路传到欧洲，最终传到了世界各地。

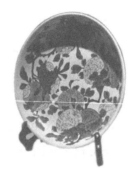

丝绸之路上的主要商品——瓷器

从中国运到西方的漂亮的丝绸和瓷器，让西方人认识了中国。也有很多外国人通过丝绸之路来到中国，并且喜欢上这里，留下来一直生活在这里。来到中国的外国人，也给中国带来了很多以前没有的东西，比如胡萝卜就是通过丝绸之路传到中国的。虽然中国人现在经常吃胡萝卜，但是大部分人却不知道它其实是从西域传进来的。除了吃的，还有更重要的东西也是经过丝绸之路传进

products to the countries on the west of China by using horses and camels. They set out from Chang'an, the capital of China at the time, and went westwards through many countries, reaching as far as the regions around the Mediterranean Sea. They sold Chinese products wherever they went.

At that time, people in Europe and Central Asia liked Chinese silk very much, but they couldn't produce it themselves, so the silk received warm welcome in these countries. As it was sold at extremely high prices, only rich people could afford it. Aside from silk, the merchants also sold

印刷术通过丝绸之路传到西方

Chinese porcelain and tea to people in the countries on the west of China.

At that time, people in the West didn't know how to make paper or how to print, but the paper-making technology and printing workmanship had already been invented by Chinese. So they were also spread along the Silk Road to Europe and finally around the world.

The beautiful silk and porcelain from China helped the people in the West learn about China. Many foreigners came to China by taking the Silk Road, liked this country and lived here permanently. These foreigners

通过丝绸之路来到中国的波斯人

佛教　Fójiào
Buddhism

宗教　zōngjiào
religion

印度　Yìndù　India

罗马　Luómǎ　Rome

航海　hánghǎi
to navigate on the sea

唯一　wéiyī
only, unique

促进　cùjìn
to promote

往来　wǎnglái
to contact

通过丝绸之路来到中国的
波斯人

来的，那就是佛教。佛教后来成了中国主要的宗教①之一，并且在很多方面影响着中国人的生活。

佛教传入中国后最早修建的白马寺，
位于河南洛阳

　　丝绸之路连接了当时世界上最发达的几个国家和地区——中国、印度、中亚和罗马时期的欧洲。当时人们还不会航海，丝绸之路成为连接东方和西方欧洲各国唯一的通道和商路，促进了这些地区经济文化上的交流和友好往来。

　　总之，丝绸之路是一条既古老又重要的商路，也是亚洲和欧洲各国经济文化交流的友谊之路。

also brought many things that China never had before, such as carrots. Though Chinese people today often eat carrots, most of them don't know that carrots were actually brought from the West. Aside from food, Buddhism, which was something much more important, was spread to China along the Silk Road. It later became one of the most important religions in China and influenced Chinese people's life in many aspects.

丝绸之路上敦煌
莫高窟里的雕像

The Silk Road connected the most developed countries and regions in the world at that time—China, India, Central Asia, and Europe of the Roman Period. In those days, people knew nothing about sea navigation. The Silk Road, the only passage and trade route connecting the East with the European countries in the West, promoted cultural and economic communication and friendship among these regions.

In summary, the Silk Road was not only an old and important trade route, but also a road of friendship helping develop the economic and cultural communications among Asian and European countries.

丝绸之路上的天水麦积山石窟

文化注释

❶ 中国的宗教

　　古代中国是个多宗教的国家，主要有佛教、道教、伊斯兰教、天主教和基督教。

◇ 练习 ◇

一 阅读理解 Reading Comprehension

练习1：判断正误 True（√）or false（×）

例 丝绸之路是中国西北部一条古老的商路。（ √ ）

1. 丝绸之路全长大约七千公里，起点是中国的新疆。（　　）

2. 丝绸之路经过甘肃、新疆，到达中亚、西亚。（　　）

3. 第一个开辟丝绸之路的人叫张骞。（　　）

4. 皇帝派张骞到西边的国家去卖丝绸。（　　）

5. 公元前 119 年，张骞第一次出使西域。（　　）

6. 丝绸之路是 19 世纪初开辟的。（　　）

7. 很多商人沿着丝绸之路，把中国的货物用马和骆驼运到西边的国家。（　　）

8. 除了丝绸，商人们还把中国的瓷器、茶叶等运到西方。（　　）

9. 中国古代的四大发明都是沿着丝绸之路传到欧洲的。（　　）

10. 从中国运到西方的漂亮的丝绸和瓷器，使西方人认识了中国。（　　）

练习 2：选择正确答案 **Choose the right answer**

例 丝绸之路是＿＿＿**B**＿＿＿一条古老的商路。

A. 中国南部　　　B. 中国西北部　　　C. 中国东部　　　D. 中国东南部

1. 丝绸之路的起点是＿＿＿＿＿＿，经过甘肃、新疆，到达中亚、西亚，进而连接＿＿＿＿＿＿各国。

A. 西安　地中海　　　　　　　B. 洛阳　亚洲

C. 西安　非洲　　　　　　　　D. 上海　地中海

2. 因为＿＿＿＿＿＿，所以这条商路就被称为"丝绸之路"。

A. 商人们都穿丝绸衣服　　　　B. 货物中丝绸产品最多、影响最大

C. 只卖丝绸　　　　　　　　　D. 丝绸很贵

3. 皇帝派张骞到西边的国家去，＿＿＿＿＿＿。

A. 增进国家之间的交往　　　　B. 开辟一条商路

C. 要求互派使节　　　　　　　D. 卖丝绸

4. 中国历史上有名的"张骞出使西域"发生在＿＿＿＿＿＿。

A. 公元前 4 世纪　　　　　　　B. 1000 年前

C. 公元 119 年　　　　　　　　D. 公元前 2 世纪

5. 张骞开辟了丝绸之路以后，中国商人就沿着这条路把＿＿＿＿＿＿运到欧洲。

A. 胡萝卜　　　B. 葡萄　　　C. 佛教　　　D. 中国的货物

6. 除了丝绸，商人们还把＿＿＿＿＿＿等运到西方，卖给当地人。

A. 书籍　　　B. 蔬菜　　　C. 胡萝卜　　　D. 瓷器、茶叶

7. ＿＿＿＿＿＿也沿着丝绸之路传到欧洲，最终传播到世界各地。

A. 造纸和印刷的方法　　　　　B. 制造火药的技术

C. 造船的技术　　　　　　　　D. 汉字的使用

8. 很多沿着丝绸之路来到中国的外国人，_____ 。

　　A. 无法跟别人交流　　　　　　　　B. 留下来生活在这里

　　C. 只喜欢丝绸　　　　　　　　　　D. 只喜欢瓷器

9. 丝绸之路也给中国带来了很多以前没有的东西，比如 _____ 。

　　A. 胡萝卜　　　　　B. 茶叶　　　　　　C. 牛羊　　　　　D. 瓷器

10. 当时 _____ ，丝绸之路是连接亚洲和欧洲各国唯一的通道和商路。

　　A. 航海很不安全　　　　　　　　　B. 还没有造船业

　　C. 人们不熟悉海路　　　　　　　　D. 人们还不会航海

■ 语句练习 Sentence-Matching Exercises

连线 **Match the left side with the information on the right**

1. 丝绸之路是一条　　　　　　　　A. 是中国汉朝的一位官员，叫张骞

2. 人们开始通过这条路　　　　　　B. 公元前 2 世纪

3. 为了增进中国和西边国　　　　　C. 所以丝绸之路是连接东西方的唯一
   家之间的交往　　　　　　　　　　　通道

4. 第一个开辟丝绸之路的人　　　　D. 并且在很多方面影响着中国人的生活

5. 张骞第一次去西域的时间是　　　E. 非常古老的商路

6. 张骞开辟了丝绸之路以后　　　　F. 最远到达过地中海地区

7. 丝绸之路从长安开始　　　　　　G. 就把中国的货物卖到哪里

8. 很多商人走到哪里　　　　　　　H. 把中国出产的货物运到欧洲

9. 佛教成了中国主要的宗教之一　　I. 中国和西域的交往越来越频繁

10. 那时候人们还不会航海　　　　　J. 皇帝派张骞去访问这些国家

三 词汇练习 Vocabulary Exercises

用课文中学过的词语填空 **Fill in the blanks with words/expressions in this lesson**

丝绸	瓷器	唯一	促进	开辟
印刷	胡萝卜	佛教	宗教	西域

　　"丝绸之路"是一条非常古老的商路。你知道谁是第一个　开辟　丝绸之路的人吗？这个人叫张骞。公元前 2 世纪，张骞带领一百多人去访问西边的国家。这就是中国历史上有名的"张骞出使＿＿＿＿＿"。张骞开辟了这条丝绸之路以后，很多商人就沿着他走过的路线，把中国的货物用马和骆驼运到西边的国家。除了＿＿＿＿，商人们还把中国的＿＿＿＿、茶叶等运到西方。造纸和＿＿＿＿的方法也是沿着丝绸之路传到欧洲的。那时候人们还不会航海，丝绸之路是连接亚洲和欧洲各国的＿＿＿＿通道。很多外国人通过丝绸之路给中国带来了以前没有的东西，比如＿＿＿＿就是那时候传到中国的。除了吃的，还有更重要的东西也是通过丝绸之路传进来的，那就是＿＿＿＿。佛教后来成了中国主要的＿＿＿＿之一。丝绸之路连接了当时世界上最发达的几个国家和地区，＿＿＿＿了这些地区经济文化上的交流和友好往来。

四 语法练习 Grammar Exercises

用所给的词语组句 **Make sentences with the words and phrases given**

例　商路　一条　是　中国西北部　丝绸之路　非常古老的

　　<u>丝绸之路是中国西北部一条非常古老的商路。</u>

1. 张骞　联系　使　中国　和　建立了　之间　第一次　西域各国

_____

2. 地中海地区　丝绸之路　最远　商人　到达过　沿着

_____

3. 造纸　传到了　的方法　世界各地　沿着　和　印刷　丝绸之路

_____

4. 运到西方的　让　从中国　漂亮的　丝绸和瓷器　西方人　认识了　中国

_____

5. 丝绸之路　唯一的　连接　和　欧洲各国的　通道　是　东方

_____

五 写作练习 Writing Practice

用下列词语造句 **Make sentences using the following words/phrases/structures**

1. 以……为……：_____

2. 进而：_____

3. 并不是……而是……：_____

4. 越来越……：_____

5. 从而：_____

6. 沿着：_____

7. 最终：_____

8. 促进了……的友好往来：_____

9. 总之：_____

10. 既……又……：_____

马可·波罗的故事

Mǎkě Bōluó, Marco Polo, a famous Italian traveler

马可·波罗和他的父亲、叔叔从欧洲来到中国

导读问题　Lead-in Questions

1. 你知道马可·波罗是怎样来到中国的吗？
2. 在中国他看到了什么？做了什么？
3. 《马可·波罗游记》是怎样写成的？
4. 这本书向欧洲人介绍了什么？
5. 这本书对欧洲人产生了什么影响？

提起　tíqǐ
to mention

威尼斯　Wēinísī
Venice

骆驼　luòtuo
camel

步行　bùxíng
to walk, to go on foot

公元　gōngyuán
Christian era

大都　Dàdū
the capital of the Yuan
Dynasty, the present-day
Beijing

大汗　dàhán
khan, emperor of the
Mongolian Empire

皇帝　huángdì
emperor

忽必烈　Hūbìliè
Kublai Khan

罗马　Luómǎ
Rome

教皇　jiàohuáng
Pope

好学　hàoxué
studious

欣赏　xīnshǎng
to appreciate

在中国，提起马可·波罗的名字，很多人都知道。

马可·波罗是世界著名的旅行家。1254年，他出生在意大利威尼斯的一个商人家庭。17岁的时候，他跟着父亲和叔叔，离开威尼斯，前往中国。路上他们有时骑马，有时骑骆驼，有时只能步行。他们翻过一座座高山，穿过一片片沙漠，克服了很多困难，花了4年多的时间，终于在1275年到达了元朝（公元1206年～公元1368年）的首都大都（今天的北京）①，见到了当时的大汗，也就是皇帝忽必烈，并拿出了罗马教皇的信和礼物。大汗还把当时三人请进皇宫，听他们讲路上发生的事情。

忽必烈接见马可·波罗（蜡像）

聪明好学的马可·波罗在路上已经学会了波斯语，到中国后又很快学会了蒙古语和汉语。大汗忽必烈非常欣赏这

In China, the name of Marco Polo is known to many people.

Marco Polo was a world-famous traveler. He was born in 1254 to a merchant family in Venice, Italy. At the age of 17, he left Venice for China with his father and his uncle. They climbed high mountains and went across deserts on horses, camels or even on foot, overcoming a lot of difficulties. It took them more than four years to finally arrive in 1275 in Dadu (the present-day Beijing), the capital of the Yuan Dynasty (1206 AD–1368 AD). They met Kublai Khan, the Emperor of the Yuan Dynasty and gave him the letter and gifts from the Roman Pope. The khan invited them to his imperial palace and asked them about what happened on their journey.

水城威尼斯

Being smart and studious, Marco Polo already learned Persian on his way. He learned Mongolian and Chinese soon after he arrived in China. The khan liked this young man very much, so he sent him on a tour of inspection around China. Taking this opportunity, Marco Polo traveled to many places around China, including Xinjiang, Gansu, Inner Mongolia, Shanxi, Shaanxi,

蒙古牧民居住的房子——蒙古包

派　pài
to send (someone on mission)

巡视　xúnshì
to make a tour of inspection

新疆　Xīnjiāng
one of the five autonomous regions in China

甘肃　Gānsù
one of the provinces in China

辽阔　liáokuò　vast

富有　fùyǒu　affluent, rich

流连忘返　liúlián wàngfǎn
to linger on

出使　chūshǐ
to serve as an envoy abroad

越南　Yuènán　Vietnam

缅甸　Miǎndiàn　Myanmar

苏门答腊　Sūméndálà
Sumatra

详细　xiángxì　detailed

考察　kǎochá
to inspect, to examine

风土人情　fēngtǔ rénqíng
folk customs

汇报　huìbào　to report

称赞　chēngzàn　to praise

能干　nénggàn
competent, capable

战争　zhànzhēng　war, battle

俘虏　fúlǔ　captire

监狱　jiānyù　prison

位年轻人，于是派他到全国各地巡视。马可·波罗利用巡视的机会，走遍了中国的山山水水。他先后去过新疆、甘肃、内蒙古、山西、陕西、四川、云南、山东、江苏、浙江、福建②以及北京等地方，中国的辽阔和富有让他流连忘返。他还出使过越南、缅甸和苏门答腊。他每到一个地方，都要详细考察当地的风土人情，回到大都后，向忽必烈汇报。对于这些情况，忽必烈都听得十分认真，称赞马可·波罗聪明能干。

元大都遗址公园

　　17年过去了，马可·波罗非常想家。花了3年多的时间，在1295年，他回到了离开多年的家乡威尼斯。之后，马可·波罗参加了一场战争，后来被俘虏。在监狱里，他和一位作家关在一起。

Sichuan, Yunnan, Shandong, Jiangsu, Zhejiang, Fujian, Beijing and other places. He was deeply impressed by China's vast territory, affluence and prosperity. Marco Polo was also sent to Vietnam, Myanmar and Sumatra as an envoy. Wherever he went, Marco

新疆风光

Polo made detailed surveys of the folk customs there and reported to the khan after returning to Dadu. Kublai Khan always listened to his words attentively and praised him for his intelligence and capability.

Seventeen years passed, and Marco Polo got very homesick. He spent over 3 years on road and finally returned to Venice, his long-separated homeland, in 1295. After that, Marco Polo became a captive in a war and was kept in captivity with a writer, to whom Marco told his experiences in China. The writer noted down and rearranged what he said, and wrote *The Travels of Marco Polo*, the first book written by a European introducing Chinese history, culture and art in detail. In this book, he presented a developed China to Europeans, highly praising China's prosperous culture, developed industry, flourishing and bustling

浙江乌镇风光

113

昌盛　chāngshèng
prosperous

繁华　fánhuá
flourishing

热闹　rènao
lively and bustling

都市　dūshì
city, metropolis

物美价廉　wù měi jià lián
inexpensive but superior

丝绸　sīchóu
silk

流通　liútōng
to circulate

想象　xiǎngxiàng
to imagine

广为流传
guǎng wéi liúchuán
widely circulated

马可·波罗雕像

马可·波罗把自己在中国的旅行经历告诉了这位作家，然后经过作家的记录和整理，写出了《马可·波罗游记》一书。这是欧洲人写的第一本详细介绍中国历史、文化和艺术的书。在《马可·波罗游记》中，他向欧洲人介绍了发达的中国，高度称赞了中国昌盛的文明、发达的工业、繁华热闹的都市、物美价廉的丝绸、完善方便的交通以及普遍流通的纸币等等，向人们展示了一个生动的中国形象。

位于江苏扬州的马可·波罗纪念馆

　　书中的内容使每一个读过这本书的人都对中国充满想象，非常向往。《马可·波罗游记》这本书被翻译成很多种语言，在世界上广为流传。很多欧洲人读了这本书以后，才发现世界的东方还有一个更文明更发达更富有的国家。书

cities, beautiful and inexpensive but superior silk, convenient transportation, and the paper currency commonly circulated around the country, and vividly presenting China to the Western people.

This book aroused every reader's imagination of and longing for China. The book was translated into many languages and became very popular around the world. Only after reading this book did many Europeans realize that there was a country in the East which

元代的瓷器

was more civilized, developed and wealthier. Marco Polo's descriptions of China in this book aroused Europeans' longing for the East, stimulating their interest in Chinese society and culture and their yearning for getting more

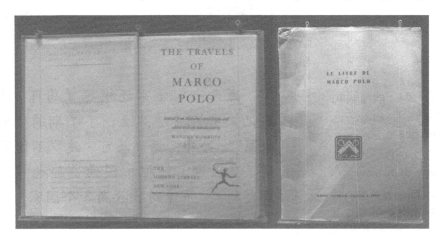

《马可·波罗游记》

115

哥伦布　Gēlúnbù
Christopher Columbus
(1451-1506), a famous
Italian navigator and
explorer

冒险　mào xiǎn
to take a risk

远航　yuǎnháng
to sail to a distant place, to
take a long voyage

探险　tànxiǎn
to explore

航海　hánghǎi
to navigate on the sea

美洲　Měizhōu
America

大陆　dàlù
mainland, continent

地理　dìlǐ　geography

描述　miáoshù
to describe

绘制　huìzhì
to draw, to map out

美食　měishí
delicacy, cuisine

中马可·波罗等人的所见所闻，激起了欧洲人对东方的热烈向往。他们开始对中国的社会和文化产生兴趣，非常渴望了解中国。著名旅行家哥伦布就是因为看了《马可·波罗游记》以后，对中国文明非常向往，才下定决心冒险远航，以实现到东方探险的愿望的。然而哥伦布的航海旅行却让他意外地发现了美洲大陆。

意大利面

西方地理学家还根据《马可·波罗游记》中的描述，绘制了早期的“世界地图”。另外，据说马可·波罗不仅人回到了意大利，还把中国的美食也带到了意大利③，并传到了欧洲各个国家。

information about China. Christopher Columbus, a famous traveler, was so attracted by the Chinese civilization after reading *The Travels of Marco Polo* that he made up his mind to go on an expedition to the East. However, his sailing on the sea led him accidentally to the discovery of the Continent of America instead.

Geographers in the West drew the early "world map" based on the descriptions in the book. In addition, it was said that Marco Polo not only returned to Italy himself, but also brought the Chinese delicacies to Italy and spread it to different European countries.

意大利比萨饼

文化注释

① 元朝首都

成吉思汗时，蒙古没有固定的首都。1235年建都哈尔和林（今蒙古国境内）。1263年，忽必烈定都上都（今内蒙古自治区正蓝旗东）。1272年定都燕京，称为大都（今北京），元朝的统治中心完全向中原转移。

② 新疆、甘肃、内蒙古、山西、陕西、四川、云南、山东、江苏、浙江、福建

新疆、内蒙古是中国的少数民族自治区，其他都是中国省份的名字。

③ 意大利美食与中国美食的关系

据说意大利许多食物都是从中国传过去的，如通心粉、比萨饼，乃至冰激凌，都是当年由著名旅行家马可·波罗传到意大利的。马可·波罗在中国旅行时最喜欢吃一种北方流行的葱油馅饼。回到意大利后他一直想再次品尝，但却不会烤制。一个星期天，他同朋友们在家中聚会，其中一位是来自那不勒斯的厨师。马可·波罗灵机一动，把那位厨师叫到身边，向他描述了中国北方的葱油馅饼。那位厨师也兴致勃勃地按马可·波罗所说的方法制作起来。但忙了半天，仍无法将馅料放入面团中。此时已快下午两点，大家都饥肠辘辘。于是马可·波罗提议就将馅料放在面饼上吃。大家品尝后，都觉得很好吃。这位厨师回到那不勒斯后又做了几次，并配上那不勒斯的乳酪和作料，大受食客们的欢迎，从此"比萨"就流传开了。

另外，据说冰激凌也是中国发明的，用羊乳酪和鸡蛋制成，藏于深山冰洞中，用于消暑。马可·波罗来到中国后，皇帝用冰激凌招待他，后来他将这种食物写进《马可·波罗游记》中，冰激凌就在欧洲流传开了。

◇ 练习 ◇

一 阅读理解 Reading Comprehension

练习 1: 判断正误 True（√）or false（×）

例 在中国，提起马可·波罗的名字，很多人都知道。（ √ ）

1. 马可·波罗来到中国的时候 17 岁。（　　　）

2. 马可·波罗他们克服了很多困难，花了 4 年多的时间到达元朝的首都大
   都。（　　　）

3. 马可·波罗学会了波斯语、藏语、蒙古语和汉语。（　　　）

4. 马可·波罗见到了蒙古帝国的大汗——成吉思汗。（　　　）

5. 大汗忽必烈非常欣赏马可·波罗，因为他是意大利人。（　　　）

6. 马可·波罗利用巡视的机会，走遍了中国的山山水水，并在很多地方做生
   意。（　　　）

7.《马可·波罗游记》是欧洲人写的第一本详细介绍中国的书。（　　　）

8.《马可·波罗游记》这本书已经被翻译成了很多种语言。（　　　）

9. 哥伦布就是因为看了《马可·波罗游记》才下定决心冒险远航的。（　　　）

10. 西方地理学家还根据书中的描述，绘制了早期的"中国地图"。（　　　）

练习 2: 选择正确答案 Choose the right answer

例 马可·波罗_____D_____的时候离开家乡前往中国。

A. 27 岁　　　　　B. 21 岁　　　　　C. 19 岁　　　　　D. 17 岁

1. 马可·波罗的故事发生在_____。

   A. 唐朝　　　　　B. 元朝　　　　　C. 明朝　　　　　D. 清朝

2. 马可·波罗跟着他的父亲和叔叔，花了_____的时间，终于来到中国。

   A. 10 年　　　　　B. 4 年多　　　　C. 17 年　　　　　D. 1 年多

3. 马可·波罗到达中国时，元朝的首都是_____。

   A. 上都　　　　　B. 长安　　　　　C. 大都　　　　　D. 威尼斯

4. 除了蒙古语和汉语以外，马可·波罗还学会了_____。

   A. 葡萄牙语　　　B. 俄语　　　　　C. 波斯语　　　　D. 藏语

5. 马可·波罗利用巡视的机会，_____。

   A. 买了很多丝绸　　　　　　B. 学会了汉语

   C. 去了缅甸和苏门答腊　　　D. 走遍了中国的山山水水

6. 每到一个地方，马可·波罗都要详细考察_____。

   A. 当地的风土人情　　　　　B. 人们的生活水平

   C. 当地的产品价格　　　　　D. 商业往来的情况

7. 17 年过去了，马可·波罗_____。花了 3 年多的时间，在 1295 年，他回到了离开多年的家乡威尼斯。

   A. 把钱花完了　　　　　　　B. 非常想家

   C. 生病了　　　　　　　　　D. 没有工作了

8. 在一位作家的帮助下，马可·波罗把_____写成了《马可·波罗游记》。

   A. 威尼斯与中国的来往　　　B. 自己与皇帝忽必烈的友谊

   C. 自己在中国的经历　　　　D. 学会的蒙古语、汉语、波斯语

9.《马可·波罗游记》是欧洲人写的第一本详细介绍 _____ 的书。

    A. 中国历史、文化和艺术　　　B. 中国与欧洲的贸易往来

    C. 皇帝　　　　　　　　　　　D. 中国地理山川

10. 很多欧洲人读了这本书以后，_____。

    A. 冒险远航到东方探险　　　　B. 对东方热烈向往

    C. 把它译成了很多种语言　　　D. 把它拍成电影

二 语句练习 Sentence-Matching Exercises

连线 **Match the left side with the information on the right**

1. 马可·波罗出生在	A. 后来被俘虏了
2. 马可·波罗跟着他的父亲和叔叔	B. 意大利威尼斯的一个商人家庭
3. 马可·波罗利用巡视的机会	C. 是欧洲人写的第一本介绍中国的书
4. 他每到一个地方	D. 激起了欧洲人对东方的热烈向往
5. 马可·波罗在 1295 年	E. 都要详细考察当地的风土人情
6. 马可·波罗参加了一场战争	F. 回到了离开多年的家乡
7. 每一个读过这本书的人	G. 来到了元朝当时的首都大都
8.《马可·波罗游记》	H. 让他意外地发现了美洲大陆
9. 哥伦布的航海旅行	I. 走遍了中国的山山水水
10. 马可·波罗等人的所见所闻	J. 都对中国充满想象，非常向往

121

三 词汇练习 Vocabulary Exercises

用课文中学过的词语填空 Fill in the blanks with words/expressions in this lesson

欣赏	巡视	骆驼	流连忘返	出使
考察	称赞	想象	远航	美食

　　马可·波罗 17 岁的时候，离开家乡前往中国。路上他们有时骑马，有时骑＿＿骆驼＿＿，有时只能步行。他们克服了很多困难，终于在 1275 年到达了元朝的首都大都。大汗忽必烈非常＿＿＿＿＿＿这位年轻人，于是派他到全国各地＿＿＿＿＿＿。他每到一个地方，都要详细＿＿＿＿＿＿当地的风土人情。中国的辽阔和富有让他＿＿＿＿＿＿。他还＿＿＿＿＿＿过越南、缅甸和苏门答腊。马可·波罗回国以后，一位作家根据他在中国的所见所闻，写出了《马可·波罗游记》。这本书向欧洲人介绍了发达的中国，高度＿＿＿＿＿＿了中国的文明昌盛。很多欧洲人读过这本书后，都对中国充满＿＿＿＿＿＿。著名旅行家哥伦布就是因为看了《马可·波罗游记》以后，对中国文明非常向往，才下定决心冒险＿＿＿＿＿＿的。据说，马可·波罗还把中国的＿＿＿＿＿＿带到了意大利。

四 语法练习 Grammar Exercises

用所给的词语组句 Make sentences with the words and phrases given

例　中国　马可·波罗　的时候　离开　17 岁　威尼斯　前往
　　马可·波罗 17 岁的时候离开威尼斯，前往中国。

1. 把　他们　皇宫　大汗　请进　路上　事情　发生的　听　讲　他们

_____

2. 考察了　马可·波罗　当地的　利用　详细地　机会　巡视的　风土人情

_____

3.《马可·波罗游记》　向　中国形象　人们　一个　展示了　生动的

_____

4. 这本书　流传　已经　很多种　被　在世界上　翻译成　语言　广为

_____

5. 东方的　马可·波罗的　欧洲人　所见所闻　热烈向往　对　激起了

_____

五 写作练习 Writing Practice

用下列词语造句 Make sentences using the following words/phrases/structures

1. 有时……有时……有时…… : _____

2. 克服 : _____

3. 流连忘返 : _____

4. 每……都…… : _____

5. 展示 : _____

6. 广为流传 : _____

7. 因为……才…… : _____

8. 下定决心：_____

9. 根据：_____

10. 据说：_____

郑和下西洋 10

Zhèng Hé, an explorer, navigator and diplomat of the Ming Dynasty

Xīyáng, West Ocean, referring to the present-day Southeast Asia, South Asia, the Middle East, Somalia and the Swahili Coast

郑和与他的船队

导读问题 Lead-in Questions

1. 明朝的皇帝（huángdì, emperor）为什么派（pài, to send [someone on mission]）郑和去海外（hǎiwài, overseas）其他国家？

2. 郑和第一次航海（hánghǎi, to navigate on the sea）是什么时候？目的是什么？

3. 郑和的船队有多少船只、多少人员？

4. 郑和的船队最远到达过哪里？

5. 郑和七次下西洋对中国与西方国家的交往有什么贡献（gòngxiàn, contribution）？

公元　gōngyuán
Christian era

成祖　Chéngzǔ
an emperor of the Ming
Dynasty

富强　fùqiáng
prosperous and strong

能干　nénggàn
capable, competent

将军　jiāngjūn
general

远航　yuǎnháng
to sail to a distant place, to
take a long voyage

指南针　zhǐnánzhēn
compass

航行　hángxíng
to sail

迷失　míshī
to get lost

造船　zào chuán
to build a ship

600 多年前，明朝（公元 1368 年~公元 1644 年）的成祖皇帝为了显示中国的富强，就派他手下一个能干的将军——郑和，远航去海外其他国家。中国历史上把这件事叫作"郑和下西洋"。

郑和下西洋

中国很早就掌握了航海技术，因为中国人最早发明了指南针，可以在大海上航行而不迷失方向，造船的技术也非常先进。早在唐朝（公元 618 年~公元 907 年），特别是宋朝（公元 960 年~公元 1279 年）、元朝（公元 1206 年~公元 1368 年）的时

郑和雕像

Over 600 years ago, Emperor Chengzu of the Ming Dynasty (1368 AD-1644 AD), to demonstrate China's prosperity, sent Zheng He, a competent general, to sail to other countries overseas. This event was known as "Zheng He Sailing to the West Ocean" in Chinese history.

造船的工人

Chinese people mastered sea navigation technology very early, because the compass, one of the Chinese inventions, ensured that people wouldn't lose their directions when sailing on the sea. They also had advanced shipbuilding technology. As early as the Tang Dynasty (618 AD–907 AD), especially in the Song Dynasty (960 AD–1279 AD) and the Yuan Dynasty (1206 AD–1368 AD), Chinese people did business with foreigners by taking the sea route, going as far as the distant regions around the Mediterranean Sea.

郑和宝船模型

海路　hǎilù
sea route

遥远　yáoyuǎn
distant, faraway

地中海　Dìzhōng Hǎi
the Mediterranean Sea

大地　dàdì
the earth, the world

尽头　jìntóu　end

巨大　jùdà
huge, mighty

率领　shuàilǐng
to lead

当时　dāngshí
at that time

水手　shuǐshǒu
sailor

士兵　shìbīng
soldier

军官　jūnguān
military officer

养活　yǎnghuo
to support, to feed

粮食　liángshi
grain

蔬菜　shūcài
vegetable

印度　Yìndù
India

候，中国人和外国人做生意主要就是走海路①，一直航行到遥远的地中海地区。

可是，这一次皇帝并不是要郑和去做生意，而是让他当"西洋大将军"，告诉他要一直航行到大地的尽头，让所有人都知道中国。

公元 1405 年，由 62 艘大海船组成的巨大船队，在郑和的率领下出发了。这是当时世界上最大的船队，船上共有 2.7 万多人，其中有水手、士兵、军官，还有翻译、商人和医生。为了养活这么多人，船上带着大量的粮食和其他各种吃的东西，而且还带了很多用来种蔬菜和水果的土和水。水里还养着鱼，游来游去。

郑和下西洋壁画

从 1405 年到 1433 年，近 30 年的时间，郑和先后七次远航。开始，他只航行到印度，后来他穿过印度洋，最远一

But Zheng He, given the title of "General of the West Ocean" by the emperor, wasn't going to do business this time, but to travel to the ends of the world to make China known to everyone.

In 1405 AD, a mighty fleet consisting of sixty-two ships set off under the leadership of Zheng He. This was the world's largest fleet of ships at that time, with over 27,000 people onboard, including sailors, soldiers, military officers, interpreters, merchants, and medical practitioners. To provide enough food for all these people, they carried on the ships a large amount of grain and a variety of food, as well as soil and water to plant vegetables and fruits. There was even water for raising fish which swam freely in it.

Zheng He made seven consecutive sea voyages from 1405 to 1433. At the beginning, he only sailed to India. Later on he went across the Indian Ocean, reaching as far as Africa. Wherever he went, he would present many gifts to the local kings. The local people were all surprised to see such a mighty fleet of ships, and willing to pay tributes to the Chinese emperor.

纪念郑和下西洋的邮票——
郑和的船队受到当地人欢迎

纪念郑和下西洋的邮票——
郑和向当地人赠送丝绸和瓷器

非洲	Fēizhōu	Africa
吃惊	chī jīng	

to be surprised

朝贡	cháogòng	

to pay tribute (to an imperial
court), to present tribute

珍珠	zhēnzhū	pearl
宝石	bǎoshí	jewel, gem
象牙	xiàngyá	ivory
香料	xiāngliào	perfume
甚至	shènzhì	even
长颈鹿	chángjǐnglù	

giraffe

扩大	kuòdà	

to enhance, to expand

亚洲	Yàzhōu	Asia
往来	wǎnglái	to contact
摆威风	bǎi wēifēng	

to show off

哥伦布	Gēlúnbù	

Christopher Columbus
(1451-1506), a famous
Italian navigator and
explorer

可惜	kěxī	regretful, sad
允许	yǔnxǔ	

to allow, to permit

下海	xià hǎi	

to go to sea

从此	cóngcǐ	

since then

直航行到了非洲。每到一个地方，他就会送给当地的国王很多礼物。当地人看到这么强大的船队，非常吃惊，都愿意向中国皇帝朝贡。

郑和的船队回中国的时候，船上装满了各种珍贵的礼物，有黄金、珍珠、宝石、象牙、香料，甚至还有一些中国人从来没有见过的特别奇怪的动物，比如长颈鹿。郑和七次下西洋，扩大了中国与亚洲、非洲各国的经济、文化往来。

但是为了这样的远航，明朝政府花了太多的钱。后来，郑和去世了，成祖皇帝也死了，新皇帝不想再花那么多钱下西洋摆威风了。

郑和下西洋比哥伦布的航行（公元1492）早了87年，并且郑和的船队要大很多，使用的技术也更先进。可惜郑和死后，明朝政府再也不允许中国人下海远航了，更不允许中国人和外国人自由交往。从此，中国向世界关上了大门②。

When Zheng He went back to China, his ships were filled with all kinds of precious gifts, including gold, pearls, jewels, ivory, perfume, and even some exotic animals Chinese had never seen before, such as giraffes. Zheng He's seven sea voyages enhanced the economic and cultural communication between China and Asian and African countries.

However, the Ming government spent too much money on these voyages. After the death of Zheng He and Emperor Chengzu, the new emperor didn't want to spend that much money on going to the West Ocean to show off any more.

Zheng He's travel to the West Ocean was 87 years earlier than Christopher Columbus's naval voyage (in 1492 AD). Moreover, he led a much larger fleet and the technology used was also much more advanced. Unfortunately, after he died, Chinese people were not allowed to make a sea voyage by Ming government any more, let alone contact freely with foreigners. Henceforth, China shut its door to the rest of the world.

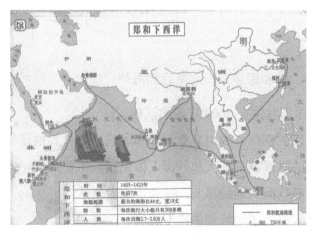

郑和航海路线图

文化注释

❶ 海上丝绸之路

  这是古代中国与外国交通贸易和文化交往的海上通道，主要有东海起航线和南海起航线两条主线路。通过海上丝绸之路往外输出的商品主要有丝绸、瓷器、茶叶和铜铁器等，往中国国内运的主要是香料、花草及一些供宫廷赏玩的奇珍异宝，所以海上丝绸之路又有海上陶瓷之路、海上香药之路之称。

❷ 闭关锁国

  指鸦片战争前中国明代、清代政府限制和禁止对外交通、贸易的政策。意思为闭关自守，不与外国往来。

◇ 练习 ◇

一 阅读理解 Reading Comprehension

练习 1：判断正误 True（ √ ）or false（ × ）

例 600 多年前，郑和跟皇帝一起航行到海外。（ × ）

1. "郑和下西洋"发生在 2000 年前的汉朝。（   ）

2. 为了显示中国的富强，成祖皇帝派郑和远航去海外其他国家。（   ）

3. 宋朝、元朝的时候，中国人和外国人做生意，主要是用船走海路。（   ）

4. 皇帝派郑和航行到大地的尽头，是为了去做生意。（   ）

5. 郑和下西洋只是为了送给别的国王礼物。（   ）

6. 船上共有 2.7 万多人，包括皇上自己。（　　　）

7. 近 30 年的时间，郑和先后七次远航。（　　　）

8. 开始，他只航行到印度，后来一直航行到了非洲。（　　　）

9. 郑和的船队回中国的时候，船上装满了珍贵的礼物。（　　　）

10. 直到清朝，中国才开始向世界关上大门。（　　　）

练习 2：选择正确答案 Choose the right answer

例 "郑和下西洋"发生在＿＿＿＿A＿＿＿＿。

    A. 明朝　　　　　B. 公元前　　　　　C. 战国时期　　　　　D. 两千年前

1. 明朝的成祖皇帝认为＿＿＿＿＿＿＿＿＿。

    A. 他的造船技术非常先进　　　　　B. 中国很富强

    C. 他是世界上唯一的皇帝　　　　　D. 中国西边没有别的国家

2. 成祖皇帝派郑和航行到海外是为了＿＿＿＿＿＿＿＿。

    A. 买珍贵的礼物　　　　　B. 做生意

    C. 显示中国的富强　　　　　D. 掌握航海技术

3. 中国人发明了＿＿＿＿＿＿＿＿＿＿，可以在大海上航行而不迷失方向。

    A. 火药　　　　　B. 航海技术　　　　　C. 指南针　　　　　D. 造船的技术

4. 郑和用了近＿＿＿＿＿＿的时间，先后七次远航。

    A. 13 年　　　　　B. 30 年　　　　　C. 18 个月　　　　　D. 10 年

5. 郑和的船队最远到达过＿＿＿＿＿＿＿。

    A. 东南亚　　　　　B. 非洲　　　　　C. 印度洋　　　　　D. 印度

6. 郑和的船上除了带着各种人员以外，还有＿＿＿＿＿＿＿＿。

    A. 明朝皇帝　　　　　B. 老师和学生

    C. 用来种蔬菜和水果的土和水　　　　　D. 长颈鹿

7. 每到一个地方，郑和就会送给当地的国王很多礼物，而当地国王也愿意向

中国皇帝_____。

A. 翻译　　　　　B. 远航　　　　　C. 往来　　　　D. 朝贡

8. 郑和的船队回中国时，船上装满了各种礼物，比如_____。

A. 香料　　　　　B. 鱼　　　　　　C. 蔬菜　　　　D. *丝绸*

9. 郑和和成祖去世后，新皇帝不想再花那么多钱下西洋_____了。

A. 朝贡　　　　　B. 摆威风　　　　C. 买宝石　　　D. 造船

10. 郑和下西洋比哥伦布的航行早了_____。

A. 78 年　　　　　B. 18 年　　　　C. 81 年　　　　D. 87 年

语句练习 Sentence-Matching Exercises

连线 **Match the left side with the information on the right**

1. "郑和下西洋" 这件事　　　　　A. 明朝政府再也不允许中国人下海远
航了

2. 当时的成祖皇帝认为　　　　　B. 而是让所有人都知道中国

3. 皇帝派郑和　　　　　　　　　C. 郑和先后七次远航

4. 宋朝和元朝的时候　　　　　　D. 后来他一直到达了非洲

5. 皇帝并不是要郑和去做生意　　E. 中国人和外国人做生意主要是走海路

6. 郑和死后　　　　　　　　　　F. 发生在 600 多年前

7. 船上带着大量的　　　　　　　G. 比哥伦布的航行早了 87 年

8. 从 1405 年到 1433 年　　　　　H. 中国是一个很富强的国家

9. 开始，郑和只航行到印度　　　I. 粮食和各种吃的东西

10. 郑和下西洋　　　　　　　　　J. 远航去海外其他国家

三 词汇练习 Vocabulary Exercises

用课文中学过的词语填空 **Fill in the blanks with words/expressions in this lesson**

指南针	珍珠	可惜	富强	翻译
珍贵	蔬菜	迷失	长颈鹿	非洲

  中国历史上著名的"郑和下西洋"发生在 600 多年前的明朝。当时的成祖皇帝为了显示中国的__富强__，派郑和远航去海外其他国家。公元 1405 年，郑和率领他的船队出发了。船队由 62 艘大海船组成，船上有_____，可以在大海上航行而不_____方向。船上共有 2.7 万多人，包括_____，所以他们可以跟别的国家的人交流。为了养活这么多人，还带了土和水，用来种_____和水果。从 1405 年到 1433 年，郑和先后七次远航，他的船队最远一直航行到_____。郑和的船队回中国的时候，船上装满了_____的礼物，有黄金、_____、宝石等等，还有中国人从来没有见过的动物，比如_____。郑和下西洋扩大了中国与亚洲、非洲各国的经济、文化往来。郑和下西洋比哥伦布的航行早了 87 年。_____郑和死后，再没有人下海远航了。

四 语法练习 Grammar Exercises

用所给的词语组句 **Make sentences with the words and phrases given**

例 去 并不是……而是…… 要 做生意 让 当 "西洋大将军"
  郑和 皇帝 他
  <u>皇帝并不是要郑和去做生意，而是让他当"西洋大将军"。</u>

1. 郑和的　率领下　在　船队　了　出发　的　组成　62 艘船　由

_____

2. 一个地方　就会　郑和　当地的　送给　每到　国王　很多礼物

_____

3. 元朝　走海路　的时候　是　做生意　和　中国人　外国人　主要

_____

4. 远航　七次　近　郑和　30 年的时间　先后

_____

5. 下西洋　哥伦布的　比　早了　航行　郑和　87 年

_____

五 写作练习 Writing Practice

用下列词语造句 Make sentences using the following words/phrases/structures

1. 为了……：_____

2. 显示：_____

3. 掌握：_____

4. 并不是……而是……：_____

5. 由……组成：_____

6. 先后：_____

7. 每……就……：_____

8. 吃惊：_____

9. 扩大：_____

10. 再也不……：_____

生词表

生词	拼音	课号
A		
安定	āndìng	2,5
安宁	ānníng	6
B		
百家言论	bǎijiā yánlùn	2
摆威风	bǎi wēifēng	10
宝石	bǎoshí	10
暴政	bàozhèng	2
爆炸	bàozhà	7
爆竹	bàozhú	7
背景	bèijǐng	1
被誉为	bèi yùwéi	3
表情	biǎoqíng	3
兵马俑	bīngmǎyǒng	3
布局	bùjú	3
步行	bùxíng	9
部落	bùluò	1
C		
才华	cáihuá	1
昌盛	chāngshèng	9
长颈鹿	chángjǐnglù	10
长生不老	chángshēng bù lǎo	7

生词	拼音	课号
朝代	cháodài	1,4,5
朝贡	cháogòng	10
朝廷	cháotíng	5
车轮	chēlún	2
称号	chēnghào	2
称赞	chēngzàn	5,6,9
成千上万	chéngqiān-shàngwàn	5
吃惊	chī jīng	10
出使	chūshǐ	1,8,9
出土	chū tǔ	3
传递	chuándì	4
瓷器	cíqì	8
磁性	cíxìng	7
从此	cóngcǐ	7,8,10
促进	cùjìn	8
D		
打败	dǎbài	2
大地	dàdì	10
大汗	dàhán	9
大将	dàjiàng	2
大陆	dàlù	9
当时	dāngshí	1,2,3,5, 6,8,10

得知	dézhī	4
地理	dìlǐ	8,9
雕塑	diāosù	5
鼎立	dǐnglì	1
都市	dūshì	5,9
度量衡	dùliànghéng	2
蹲	dūn	3

F

发掘	fājué	3
翻飞	fānfēi	7
繁华	fánhuá	9
繁荣	fánróng	1,5
防御	fángyù	2,4
分裂	fēnliè	1
风俗习惯	fēngsú xíguàn	8
风土人情	fēngtǔ rénqíng	9
封建	fēngjiàn	1
烽火台	fēnghuǒtái	4
锋利	fēnglì	3
佛法	fófǎ	6
佛经	fójīng	6
佛像	fóxiàng	5
服从	fúcóng	2
服饰	fúshì	3

俘虏	fúlǔ	9
富强	fùqiáng	10
富有	fùyǒu	9

G

感人	gǎnrén	6
高僧	gāosēng	6
格律	gélǜ	5
工程	gōngchéng	3,5
工艺	gōngyì	3,5,7
弓	gōng	3
公元	gōngyuán	1,2,4,5, 7,8,9,10
功过	gōngguò	2
攻击	gōngjī	7
宫殿	gōngdiàn	3
贡献	gòngxiàn	2,6,7,10
古老	gǔlǎo	8
古体诗	gǔtǐshī	5
固定	gùdìng	5,7
关键词	guānjiàncí	7
观赏	guānshǎng	4
官员	guānyuán	2,8
光滑	guānghuá	7
广为流传	guǎng wéi liúchuán	9
轨道	guǐdào	2

国力	guólì	5
国土	guótǔ	1

H		
海路	hǎilù	10
海外	hǎiwài	1,5,10
航海	hánghǎi	7,8,9,10
航海家	hánghǎijiā	1
航行	hángxíng	7,10
好学	hàoxué	9
后世	hòushì	2
皇帝	huángdì	1,2,3,4,6,8,9,10
黄金时代	huángjīn shídài	5
回访	huífǎng	8
汇报	huìbào	9
绘画	huìhuà	1,5
绘制	huìzhì	9
混合	hùnhé	7
活埋	huómái	2
活跃	huóyuè	2
活字印刷术	huózì yìnshuāshù	1,7
火药	huǒyào	1,7
货币	huòbì	1,2
货物	huòwù	8

J		
级别	jíbié	3
记载	jìzǎi	1,5
加热	jiārè	7
家喻户晓	jiāyù-hùxiǎo	6
甲骨文	jiǎgǔwén	1
监狱	jiānyù	9
简化	jiǎnhuà	2
建造	jiànzào	3,4,6
建筑	jiànzhù	4
剑	jiàn	3
将军	jiāngjūn	3,10
浆	jiāng	7
叫唤	jiàohuan	3
教皇	jiàohuáng	9
尽头	jìntóu	10
近体诗	jìntǐshī	5
惊叹	jīngtàn	3
惊讶	jīngyà	3
精细	jīngxì	1
景象	jǐngxiàng	1
久远	jiǔyuǎn	3
局面	júmiàn	1
举世闻名	jǔshì wénmíng	2

举头	jǔ tóu	5		辽阔	liáokuò	9
巨大	jùdà	7,10		陵墓	língmù	3
绝句	juéjù	5		流传	liúchuán	2,4
军官	jūnguān	10		流连忘返	liúlián wàngfǎn	9
军事	jūnshì	1,3		流通	liútōng	2,9
军事家	jūnshìjiā	1		硫磺	liúhuáng	7
郡	jùn	2		律诗	lùshī	5

K

				罗盘	luópán	7
开采	kāicǎi	7		骆驼	luòtuo	8,9

开创	kāichuàng	1

M

开辟	kāipì	8		埋	mái	3
开通	kāitōng	1		冒险	mào xiǎn	9
铠甲	kǎijiǎ	3		美食	měishí	9
考察	kǎochá	9		迷失	míshī	7,10
可惜	kěxī	10		棉衣	miányī	4
坑	kēng	3		描述	miáoshù	9
空前	kōngqián	5		名录	mínglù	3,4
控制	kòngzhì	1		命令	mìnglìng	2
脍炙人口	kuàizhì-rénkǒu	5		模仿	mófǎng	3
扩大	kuòdà	5,10		木炭	mùtàn	7

L

N

连接	liánjiē	1,2,4,8		内地	nèidì	2
炼	liàn	7		能干	nénggàn	9,10
粮食	liángshi	10		泥塑	nísù	5

奴隶制	núlìzhì	1

O

偶然	ǒurán	3

P

拍电影	pāi diànyǐng	6
排列	páiliè	3,7
排律	páilǜ	5
派	pài	2,8,9,10
陪葬	péizàng	3
频繁	pínfán	8
品种	pǐnzhǒng	5
平方米	píngfāngmǐ	3
屏障	píngzhàng	4
破布	pò bù	7

Q

奇迹	qíjì	3
起点	qǐdiǎn	4,8
前所未有	qiánsuǒwèiyǒu	1,5
枪炮	qiāngpào	7
强盛	qiángshèng	1,5
钦佩	qīnpèi	6
侵犯	qīnfàn	2,4
取经	qǔ jīng	6
权力	quánlì	2

R

热闹	rènao	9
任命	rènmìng	2
日日夜夜	rìrìyèyè	4

S

僧人	sēngrén	6
商路	shānglù	8
少数民族	shǎoshù mínzú	1
深远	shēnyuǎn	2
神龙	shénlóng	7
神奇	shénqí	7
甚至	shènzhì	5,6,10
胜地	shèngdì	4
盛世	shèngshì	1,5
诗歌	shīgē	1,5
诗人	shīrén	1,5
石雕	shídiāo	5
使命	shǐmìng	6
使者	shǐzhě	8
始	shǐ	2
士兵	shìbīng	3,4,10
世	shì	2
世世代代	shìshìdàidài	2
世袭制	shìxízhì	1

市区	shìqū	4
是非	shìfēi	2
手工业	shǒugōngyè	5
守护	shǒuhù	3
守卫	shǒuwèi	4
首领	shǒulǐng	1
书法	shūfǎ	1
蔬菜	shūcài	10
树皮	shùpí	7
率领	shuàilǐng	1,8,10
霜	shuāng	5
水利	shuǐlì	5
水手	shuǐshǒu	10
丝绸	sīchóu	1,8,9
私自	sīzì	6
寺庙	sìmiào	6

T

谈论	tánlùn	2,6
探险	tàn xiǎn	9
陶器	táoqì	5
陶俑	táoyǒng	3
特产	tèchǎn	5
提起	tíqǐ	5,7,9
挑选	tiāoxuǎn	6

同类	tónglèi	5
铜盘	tóngpán	7
统一	tǒngyī	1,2,3,4

W

往来	wǎnglái	2,8,10
威信	wēixìn	2
唯一	wéiyī	8
物产	wùchǎn	8
物美价廉	wù měi jià lián	9

X

下海	xià hǎi	10
仙丹	xiāndān	7
鲜艳	xiānyàn	5
县	xiàn	2
相互	xiānghù	2,8
香料	xiāngliào	10
详细	xiángxì	1,8,9
想象	xiǎngxiàng	3,9
象牙	xiàngyá	10
硝石	xiāoshí	7
欣赏	xīnshǎng	6,9
雄伟	xióngwěi	4,5
修建	xiūjiàn	1,4,5
修筑	xiūzhù	2

栩栩如生	xǔxǔ rú shēng	3	造纸	zào zhǐ	8
巡视	xúnshì	9	造纸术	zàozhǐshù	1,7
Y			增进	zēngjìn	8
烟花	yānhuā	7	战争	zhànzhēng	1,2,7,9
延续	yánxù	1,2	珍珠	zhēnzhū	10
沿用	yányòng	5	政权	zhèngquán	1
沿着	yánzhe	5,8	政治	zhèngzhì	1,2,8
养蚕业	yǎngcányè	1	指南针	zhǐnánzhēn	1,7,10
养活	yǎnghuo	10	指向	zhǐxiàng	7
遥远	yáoyuǎn	10	制度	zhìdù	2
耀眼	yàoyǎn	7	治理	zhìlǐ	1,2
遗产	yíchǎn	3,4	周长	zhōucháng	3
印刷	yìnshuā	7,8	诸侯国	zhūhóuguó	2
勇往直前	yǒngwǎng-zhíqián	4	逐渐	zhújiàn	2
悠久	yōujiǔ	7	煮	zhǔ	7
游览	yóulǎn	4	转动	zhuàndòng	7
友谊	yǒuyì	8	壮观	zhuàngguān	4,5
原型	yuánxíng	6	壮美	zhuàngměi	7
远航	yuǎnháng	9,10	姿势	zīshì	3
云海	yúnhǎi	7	字盘	zìpán	7
允许	yǔnxǔ	5,10	宗教	zōngjiào	8
Z			最终	zuìzhōng	8
造船	zào chuán	10	做工	zuògōng	3,5

专有名词

生词	拼音	课号
A		
阿富汗	Āfùhàn	6
B		
八达岭	Bādá Lǐng	4
巴基斯坦	Bājīsītǎn	6
白居易	Bái Jūyì	1,5
扁鹊	Biǎnquè	1
C		
蔡伦	Cài Lún	7
曹操	Cáo Cāo	1
长安	Cháng'ān	5,6,8
陈胜	Chén Shèng	2
成吉思汗	Chéngjísī Hán	1
成祖	Chéngzǔ	10
D		
大都	Dàdū	9
地中海	Dìzhōng Hǎi	8,10
杜甫	Dù Fǔ	1,5
F		
非洲	Fēizhōu	1,10
佛教	Fójiào	6,8

生词	拼音	课号
G		
甘肃	Gānsù	8,9
甘肃省	Gānsù Shěng	4
哥伦布	Gēlúnbù	9,10
古北口	Gǔběikǒu	4
H		
汉武帝	Hàn Wǔdì	1
河北省	Héběi Shěng	4
忽必烈	Hūbìliè	9
黄崖关	Huángyá Guān	4
J		
嘉峪关	Jiāyù Guān	4
金山岭	Jīnshān Lǐng	4
K		
康熙	Kāngxī	1
孔子	Kǒngzǐ	1
L		
老子	Lǎozǐ	1
李白	Lǐ Bái	1,5
李世民	Lǐ Shìmín	1
刘邦	Liú Bāng	1
罗马	Luómǎ	5,8,9

	M	
马可·波罗	Mǎkě Bōluó	1,9
满族	Mǎnzú	1
美洲	Měizhōu	9
蒙古族	Měnggǔzú	1
孟姜女	Mèngjiāngnǚ	4
孟子	Mèngzǐ	1
缅甸	Miǎndiàn	9
慕田峪	Mùtián Yù	4

	N	
南亚	Nányà	6

	Q	
启	Qǐ	1
乾隆	Qiánlóng	1
秦国	Qínguó	2,3
秦始皇	Qín Shǐhuáng	1,2,3,4
秦始皇陵	Qín Shǐhuáng Líng	3
屈原	Qū Yuán	1

	S	
三国演义	Sānguó Yǎnyì	1
沙和尚	Shā héshang	6
山海关	Shānhǎi Guān	4
史记	Shǐjì	1
司马迁	Sīmǎ Qiān	1

司马台	Sīmǎtái	4
丝绸之路	Sīchóu Zhī Lù	1,5,8
苏门答腊	Sūméndálà	9
孙悟空	Sūn Wùkōng	6
孙子	Sūnzǐ	1

	T	
唐僧	Tángsēng	6
唐太宗	Táng Tàizōng	1,6
天津	Tiānjīn	4
天竺	Tiānzhú	6

	W	
威尼斯	Wēinísī	9
吴承恩	Wú Chéng'ēn	6
吴道子	Wú Dàozǐ	5
吴广	Wú Guǎng	2
武则天	Wǔ Zétiān	1

	X	
西天	Xītiān	6
西亚	Xīyà	1,5,8
西洋	Xīyáng	1,10
西游记	Xīyóu Jì	6
西域	Xīyù	1,8
咸阳	Xiányáng	3
新疆	Xīnjiāng	8,9

145